The Elementary School of the Future

A Focus on Community

Edwin T. Merritt
James A. Beaudin
Jeffrey A. Sells
Richard S. Oja

Published in partnership with Fletcher-Thompson, Inc., and
the Association of School Business Officials International

ScarecrowEducation
Lanham, Maryland • Toronto • Oxford

Published in partnership with Fletcher-Thompson, Inc., and
the Association of School Business Officials International

Published in the United States of America
by ScarecrowEducation
An imprint of The Rowman & Littlefield Publishing Group, Inc.
4501 Forbes Boulevard, Suite 200, Lanham, Maryland 20706
www.scarecroweducation.com

PO Box 317
Oxford
OX2 9RU, UK

British Library Cataloguing in Publication Information Available

Library of Congress Cataloging-in-Publication Data

The elementary school of the future : a focus on community / Edwin T. Merritt ... [et al.].—
    1st ScarecrowEducation ed.
        p. cm.
    "Published in partnership with Fletcher-Thompson, Inc., and the Association of School
Business Officials International."
    Includes bibliographical references.
    ISBN 1-57886-100-4 (pbk. : alk. paper)
    1. Elementary school facilities—United States—Planning. 2. Elementary school
    buildings—United States—Planning. 3. Education—Effect of technological innovations
    on—United States. 4. Elementary school education—United States—History. I. Merritt,
    Edwin T., 1936–

LB3209.E54 2004
372.16'21—dc22

                                                        2003063289

The Elementary School of the Future
A Focus on Community

by
Edwin T. Merritt, Ed.D., Director of Educational Planning and Research
James A. Beaudin, AIA, Principal, Education Practice Group
Jeffrey A. Sells, AIA, Senior Design Architect
and Richard S. Oja, AIA, Senior Project Manager

Fletcher-Thompson, Inc.
Bridgeport and Hartford, Connecticut, and Edison, New Jersey

with
Karen Fairbanks and Scott Marble
Marble Fairbanks Architects, New York City
and
Barry Blades, ASLA
Blades & Goven Landscape Architects, Shelton, Connecticut

and additional contributions by
Joseph G. Costa, AIA
Daniel Davis
L. Gerald Dunn, R.A.
John D. Jenney
Julie A. Kim, AIA
Patricia A. Myler, AIA
JoAnne Nardone, Ed. D.
John C. Oliveto, P.E.
Marcia T. Palluzzi, LA
Robert J. Poletto, P.E.
Edward Weber, P.E.

Acknowledgments

Many people contributed their talents, skills, wisdom, and experience to this book. First, we would like to express our deep thanks to the principals of Fletcher-Thompson, Inc., for their willingness to support the book's production and their recognition of its importance.

We are especially grateful for the valuable contributions made by the principals of the two other firms participating in this project: Karen Fairbanks and Scott Marble of Marble Fairbanks Architects, New York City, and Barry Blades, of Blades & Goven Landscape Architects, Shelton, Connecticut. This book would be much poorer without their exciting and insightful work.

We also extend thanks to Dr. JoAnne Nardone, Principal of the Milton School, Rye, New York; to Dr. Ed Shine, Superintendent of the Rye City Schools; and to the Rye Board of Education for permitting us to publish the educational specification that appears in Chapter 4. Thanks are due, as well, to the many citizens of Rye—including educators, administrators, and parents—who participated in that exemplary document's development.

Fletcher Thompson administrative assistants Marie Fennessy and Joyce A. Saltes provided invaluable help and always found time to help move the project along. The many members of the Fletcher Thompson staff who participated directly in this book's creation by authoring chapters or contributing ideas or written text to various sections of the book are credited as co-authors and have our great thanks. Over time, the entire Fletcher Thompson Educational Practice Group has become involved in this series, and all have exhibited patience and enthusiasm on the many occasions when the books in our "Schools of the Future" series have gotten in the way of revenue-producing work.

Fletcher Thompson graphic designers Andy Krochko and Brian Russo, with the assistance of Marketing Coordinator Jan Pasqua, deserve our thanks and compliments for their great design and hard work in formatting the book. Marketing Coordinator Diane Kozel was always ready to help with the many details that go into a book's production.

We are grateful, too, for the enthusiasm shown for this project by Managing Editor Cindy Tursman and the staff of ScarecrowEducation, as well as the Association of School Business Officials, and we look forward to continuing our superb working relationship as we bring the other volumes in this series to publication.

And, most important, a large thank-you to James Waller, of Thumb Print New York, Inc., who demonstrated his good humor and editorial skill in scoping the contents of this book, organizing the material, and putting the text into readable shape.

Preface

When a community decides to build a new public elementary school, it is taking on a task that is sure to be lengthy, complicated, and expensive. And the job of bringing a new school facility into being is, today, made even more daunting by the fact the nature of education is changing so rapidly. The expanding role that technology plays in schooling our children is, of course, a major force behind these changes. But technology is not the only driver of change. As policymakers and the American people debate the future course of public education in this country, a very wide gamut of issues is influencing—or should be influencing—the ways in which new elementary schools are conceived, planned, funded, designed, built, and used.

These issues, to choose just a few, range from large questions concerning the general approach we should take in educating students; to specific questions of curriculum; to concerns about safety and security; to the pressure exerted on finances and facilities by rising enrollments; to the need to conform to burgeoning federal, state, and local laws and regulations enacted to meet the needs of special-education students; to the desire to define the role that elementary school buildings play in addressing the facility needs of the wider community.

We at Fletcher-Thompson, Inc.—architects, engineers, interior designers, and educators—plan and design educational facilities. Although the firm is not directly involved in educating students, our long and varied experience in the design of school buildings leads us to understand that each of the issues contributing to the current debate over the future of American public education has—or should have—a substantial impact on how schools are designed and engineered. We say "should be" and "should have," above, because it is our belief that, all too often, this complex of issues is given too little attention in the process by which schools are planned, funded, designed, and built today.

To plan the elementary school of the future—one that will truly accommodate the educational needs of five, ten, or fifteen years from now—requires a comprehensive vision. In compiling this book—which we hope will reach state officials, superintendents and other school-district administrators, local boards of education, principals, teachers, parents, and taxpayers—we at Fletcher-Thompson are attempting to begin articulating such a vision. Our point of view is that of designers who have had the privilege of helping to create school buildings across New England and beyond. But we hope that by gathering together information on the major issues likely to affect elementary school design in the years to come—and by outlining a new collaborative process for the creation of genuinely forward-looking elementary school facilities—we will be providing real, practical help to communities across America that are now engaged in setting their future educational agendas.

——*Edwin T. Merritt, James A. Beaudin, Jeffrey A. Sells, and Richard S. Oja*
Shelton and Hartford, Connecticut, July 2003

Foreword

Think About It *Today*: The Need for a Pragmatic Futurist Approach To School Planning and Design

By Edwin T. Merritt, Ed.D.

We can't stop the future from happening. We're moving into it, every moment of our lives. The future belongs to us, but, more than that, it belongs to *our children.*

These are simple, inarguable truths. So why is it that the future is so often ignored—or given very short shrift—in school planning and design? I can think of several, related reasons.

First of all, it can be *difficult* to think about the future. Not only is the future unpredictable (we all know that), but getting even a limited grasp on the kinds of developments the future might bring requires us to know something about the many trends and forces that are shaping human life right now. That's quite a large field—and so it's no wonder that people feel intimidated before they even begin. Understanding and solving *today's* problems seems challenging enough. Who has the time or energy to think about the future?

Second, thinking about the future can be . . . well, it can be a little *scary.* We Americans are in love with technology; we're thrilled by scientific and technical advances, and we're very quick to welcome the latest innovations—whether they're new features on our cell phones or new gizmos in the doctor's office. But that pleasure is just one facet of what we feel toward technology. Technical advances also frustrate, concern, and—yes—frighten us. The complexity of this emotion is perfectly reasonable. "Technology" doesn't just mean cell phones and MRIs; it means cloning and genetically modified food and sophisticated weapons systems and corporate Big Brothers reading your mind every time you make a credit-card purchase. No wonder our feelings are so mixed—and no wonder that, when asked to think about the future, we so often take refuge in the Scarlett O'Hara syndrome: "I'll think about it *tomorrow.*"

Third, planning for the future can seem *expensive,* or financially risky. We sometimes feel that people who want to talk to us about the future are trying to sell us a bill of goods, trying to get us to shell out for costly things that we may never really need—or that will become obsolete before we ever get around to learning how to use them. It goes without saying that this kind of fear—that by thinking about the future, we're opening ourselves up to being taken for a ride—grows more intense during a time of economic instability, when every financial outlay has to be carefully justified.

Finally, thinking about the future can seem *impractical.* For hundreds—perhaps thousands—of years, people have been making predictions about the future that simply haven't come true, or that have come true in ways so very different from what the prophets imagined that it more or less amounts to the same thing. The actual year 1984 didn't look at all like the world predicted in George Orwell's 1949 novel. Y2K was a well-publicized bust, and the year 2001—the setting for Stanley Kubrick's 1968 *Space Odyssey*—passed without out any earthling actually engaging in interplanetary travel.

And even when the predictions have been accurate, they've only been partly so. If you'd gone to the "Futurama" exhibit at the 1939 New York World's Fair, you'd have seen the world of 1960 as envisioned by the automakers at General Motors; their vision got some things right—the freeways, the highway cloverleafs—but it also got a lot wrong (the GM folks neglected to mention the rush-hour traffic jams, or the fact that the flight to the suburbs permitted by the automobile would wreak havoc on our cities). Because so little of what I or anyone has to say about the future may come true, anyway—or may "come true" in a way so different from what we envision—why bother to listen?

So, since thinking about the future is so hard, so scary, and so difficult to justify economically, let's not rush right into it. Instead, let's approach the matter "through the backdoor," so to speak, spending a little time thinking about the past and the present—particularly as they relate to the ways we've educated (and continue to educate) our children and to the school buildings we send them to, expecting them to learn.

Backward-Looking Education?

As someone once said, "The past is prologue," and there's no better way to get a handle on the importance of thinking about the future when planning new schools than to examine how well the school facilities built over the past half-century have accommodated the "future." (The future, that is, that's already passed or passing.)

Let's be clear: I'm *not* talking about school buildings that are in bad shape, physically (though there are lots of those, obviously, and there's a crying need for a program of national scope to repair, upgrade, and in many cases replace deteriorating school facilities). I'm talking about *well-maintained schools* in *affluent* school districts. How well have such facilities responded to the great changes that have occurred—technologically and otherwise—in American education over, say, the past 20 years? How well have they adapted to social, economic, and other changes impacting education?

The short answer is: *not* very well.

Let's begin with the very simplest sort of example. The *New York Times* recently reported on a number of Connecticut public high schools that have been forced to restrict the privilege of driving to school to seniors, leaving junior-year drivers grumbling about the indignity—the "uncoolness"—of having to return to taking the bus to and from school each day (Gross 2003). The reason for this harsh new restriction: there's no room for all the cars. This, obviously, is more a social than an educational problem per se, and it's obviously a problem that could only afflict an extremely wealthy society, but it points up something noteworthy. All over the country, high school parking lots are groaning, bursting at the seams from an onslaught of private vehicles—a crisis (of sorts) that these schools' planners and designers never imagined. Snarled traffic has become the norm even at many suburban elementary and middle schools, as parents have increasingly taken to dropping their children off and picking them up rather than relying on the school bus. *Could* yesterday's school planners have anticipated this situation, and taken steps to alleviate it? Perhaps not, but it's certainly an interesting question.

So let's turn our attention to another current space-related issue, one that bears more directly on the educational experience itself. This issue has to do with books. Printed books are physical objects—they take up space. Today, school media centers (which in the days before the "information revolution" used to be known as *libraries*) are, with rare exceptions, designed to store many, many books. They have lots of bookshelves, lots of what librarians call "stack space." So what's wrong with that? We want our schoolchildren to have access to lots of information, right? And doesn't that mean lots of books (and lots of space to store them)?

Well, not quite. Few people seriously doubt that books—printed books— have great value, or that the technology of the printed book, which has been with us ever since Gutenberg, will remain a useful technology for years and years to come. The issue is that, over the past few decades, books—and, for that matter, other printed information sources, like magazines and newspapers—have been supplemented by a wide range of other technologies for conveying and accessing text-based information. *Electronic* technologies.

We all know this. We use these technologies every day. And we know, too, that for many purposes electronic technologies are superior to books as repositories of information. Which is better? A multivolume printed encyclopedia or an online encyclopedia? The "real" encyclopedia takes up several feet of shelf space and gathers dust when it's not being used. It can be physically damaged, and each of its volumes can be used by only one reader at a time. What's more, the pace of advance in scientific and technical fields is so rapid that a printed reference work like this is almost guaranteed to be out of date in certain important respects even before the ink is dry. And obsolescence doesn't just apply to the scientific and technical information such a work contains. Geographical information becomes quickly obsolete (an encyclopedia published in 1991 would have had a long article on the "Soviet Union"). History in all its dimensions—artistic, biographical, cultural, political—continues to unfold, which means that information on the arts, people, governments, and so on all needs to be constantly updated.

A virtual encyclopedia, unlike its tangible, physical cousin, has none of these drawbacks. It takes up no storage space—or not, at least, at the point of access. Its "pages" can't get dog-eared (or cut out); it has no spine to break. It can be used by multiple researchers simultaneously. It can be rapidly and continuously updated. What's more, it can be searched—"mined" might be the better word—for information in a much more thorough, much more creative way than a printed reference work. It can be interactive. And, as if all that weren't enough to convince us of its superiority, subscribing to such an online reference is likely to be vastly cheaper than having to replace that heavy, hardbound printed set every couple of years.

As I say, we all know this. Students today are very much in the habit of taking advantage of electronic resources like the online encyclopedia I've just described (and many, many other such resources besides). *Why* is it, then, that we're still designing media centers to accommodate lots and lots and lots of printed materials? Why are we still dedicating all that valuable, expensive square footage to storage space that, as the years go on, will be less and less necessary?

We all recognize that schools designed even a decade or two ago have in many cases adapted only very uncomfortably to the technological revolution that has so recently transformed virtually every aspect of education. We're all familiar with learning spaces—including media centers—into which computers and other electronic technologies have been "squeezed" in ways that are not very ergonomic and not very aesthetically satisfying, and, most important, in ways that inhibit rather than enhance flexibility. So why do we still design and build new school facilities in ways that probably won't serve future purposes very well?

One reason, certainly, is that we are creatures of habit. We often have trouble seeing the changes that *are* taking place—that *have already* taken place—much less those that lie ahead. We often can't see that solutions to our problems are right at our fingertips.

Let's stay on the subject of printed books for a moment. In December 2002, the *New York Times* carried a story about parents in California and elsewhere around the country who are raising Cain about the weight of all the textbooks that their children are being forced to carry to and from school each day (Dillon 2002). Textbooks have gotten bigger and bigger, heavier and heavier: the story tells of one mother who weighed her daughter's textbook-stuffed backpack, which came in at 28 pounds. Another mother reported that her son's daily textbook burden amounted to 42 pounds. In districts that have eliminated lockers because of concerns about weapons and drugs, the burden on schoolchildren's backs is even greater, since they must lug the books around with them all day long. Backpacks, it seems, are *literally* bursting at the seams; the parents interviewed were of course concerned about the effect of carrying all this weight on their children's long-term health, but they were also angry about the cost of having to replace torn backpacks every few months.

The story mentioned several proposed solutions to the problem: make textbooks lighter-weight; divide them up into multiple (and smaller) volumes; issue students two sets of books—one for use in school, the other for use at home; allow students to bring wheeled packs to school; bring back school lockers in those districts that have eliminated them. What's so interesting here is that the *best* possible solution appears never to have crossed the minds of those parents, educators, and legislators who were interviewed for the story: *Why not just eliminate printed textbooks entirely and replace them with electronic books or other, Web-based products?* The technology for solving the problem already exists, *has* existed for a long time. Why not use it?

Now, granted, there are economic interests at stake here. The publishing companies that produce printed textbooks would have to come up with alternative electronic products. Textbook printers and distributors would no doubt suffer a sharp decline in business. School districts would have to take steps to ensure that each schoolchild could access electronic resources at home. And so on. But changing our basic ways of doing things always has some economic consequences, and in this case it's hard to see how those consequences, as a whole, would be worse than the consequences of what we're now doing—which is virtually guaranteeing that a whole generation of children grows up with musculoskeletal problems resulting from lugging all that weight around.

Now, let's turn our attention away from that old-fashioned technology—paper-and-ink—back to "current" technology (i.e., the computer). Why have I put those quotation marks around "current"? Why, simply because—as we're all aware—computer and computer-related technologies change so quickly that it's very dangerous to describe something as "current." The almost brand-new iMac on which this is being written has a storage capacity of 80 gigabytes—a capacity that would've been unimaginable in a home computer just a few short years ago. What's more, it's networked, wirelessly, to another home computer, a remote printer, and so on. It's perpetually connected to the Internet via cable-TV cable, and access to the Web is virtually instantaneous. Wow, huh?

Well, as you and I both know, such a home setup is hardly unusual these days. And, if you're reading this five or even two years hence, you're probably not thinking, "Wow!" You're probably thinking, "Gee, what a puny little machine. And what a primitive little network!"

I'm hardly trying to brag about how "wired" (or "wirelessly wired"?) I am. The point I'm working toward is that—knowing all we do about the rapidity of change in the arena of computer technology—we continue to design schools for *today's* technology (or even yesterday's), not tomorrow's. There are, of course, some new schools that have been designed in technologically savvy, future-oriented ways, but there are plenty of others whose design is based on the "state of the art" of five or even ten years ago. Face it: Hardwired computer stations and dedicated computer labs—no matter how well integrated into an overall design—begin to look positively antique in an era when students are carrying cell phones and PDAs that enable them to connect wirelessly, effortlessly, and oh-so portably to the Internet.

In fact, we're not even fully exploiting the *wired* technologies that we have. In many cases, high school science-lab suites are still being designed in ways that don't realize the space- and cost-saving possibilities conferred by virtual laboratory environments—which are now quite sophisticated, highly interactive, and every bit as good for teaching the experimental method, especially in the lower high school grades, as their "real life" equivalents. And we're certainly not utilizing distance-learning and teleconferencing technologies (which already exist) to the fullest extent possible, which would allow schools, districts, regions, and even statewide school systems to share resources more effectively, cutting costs and (probably) enabling space reductions in individual schools.

I should go a step further, here, and say that it isn't at all difficult to imagine the space-related implications of a situation in which all of a school's students (and faculty, and staff) have immediate, personal, wireless, fully portable access to a full range of electronic information resources. This kind of situation—and we're not very far from getting there—would, very simply, eliminate the need for the various sorts of dedicated computer spaces that are still being designed and built into new schools today.

Parking lots. Printed books. Information technology. So far, I haven't even touched on the core aspects of the educational experience—the curriculum itself, the instructional methods used, socialization dynamics, the ways schools are organized (and the ways they make decisions)—or on how these central aspects of education, as they exist today, do or do not relate to today's and tomorrow's realities.

I've just been reading an intriguing little book (you see, I do appreciate the value of paper-and-ink technology!) called *Tomorrow Now: Envisioning the Next Fifty Years,* by futurist Bruce Sterling. Let's listen to Sterling's trenchant take on contemporary American education and its relevance to the world outside the schoolhouse. "My older daughter," Sterling writes

> is a student in high school. . . . [S]he lives in harsh paramilitary constraint. She has a dress code. She fills out permission forms and tardy slips, stands in lines, eats in a vast barracks mess room. She comes and goes at the jangle of a bell, surrounded by hall monitors. . . . My child leads a narrow, tough, archaic working life. Though she isn't paid for her efforts, she'd do pretty well as a gung-ho forties-era Rosie the Riveter. . . .
>
> Today's schoolchildren are held to grueling nineteenth-century standards. Today's successful adults learn constantly, endlessly developing skills and moving from temporary phase to phase, much like preschoolers. Children are in training for stable roles in large, paternalistic bureaucracies. These enterprises no longer exist for their parents. . . .
>
> Today's young students are being civilized for an older civilization than their own. . . .
>
> It's no coincidence that my daughter is appalled by her schoolwork but thrilled by the Internet. Loathing her official school

assignments, she spends hours tracking down arcana on the Net, in patient orgies of pop-culture research. (Sterling 2002, pp. 42–44)

Now, certainly Sterling is exaggerating for effect, and he's generalizing from his own child's experience—or his impression of it—to make claims about the experience of all schoolchildren in America today. I'm an educator, and so I know that there's lots that's right about American education, and that conditions in many schools aren't nearly so harsh or so "archaic" as Sterling would have us believe. But, even so, the overall point he's making has some real validity. The enforced routines his daughter is made to follow in school are backward-looking; they have precious little to do with the world outside school—or with the workworld she'll ultimately enter. That workworld's values include an extremely high degree of flexibility, intensive teamwork, the ability to think and act effectively "on your feet" and in "nonlinear" modes. The contemporary and future workworld is (and I'll use a big word here) *protean*—as is the valued employee in that world of work. "Protean" means constantly changing, constantly shifting, constantly *adapting*—and nothing could be further from the inflexible, regimented routines that Sterling's daughter has to endure.

It's clear that that backward-looking approach to education *has* to change.

A Critical Juncture

American public education has reached a critical juncture in its history. The trouble is, the situation is confusing, and no one really knows which of several directions we'll eventually end up moving in. It's likely, in fact, that we'll continue moving in several different directions simultaneously. Let me give some examples.

On the one hand, a concern for diminishing performance in reading, math, and science skills is leading us, as a nation, toward greater standardization in curriculum, with an emphasis on evaluating every schoolchild's performance—and that of every school and school district—through standardized testing. This approach, epitomized in the No Child Left Behind Act passed by Congress and championed by the Bush administration, has its virtues—it demonstrates real concern for academic excellence—and it has many advocates.

At the same time that there's this push toward standardized curricula and standardized testing, however, there's a movement in what seems to be the opposite direction: toward highly exploratory, individualized (and individually directed) learning. There are, for example, teachers, parents, and students across the country who are railing against the practice of "teaching to the test," which, in their view, sucks the life (and a great deal of the value) out of the educational experience. There's the gathering strength of the middle school movement—treated in great detail in another volume of this "Schools of the Future" series—which has always emphasized a highly exploratory, highly interactive educational experience for young adolescents. There's the fact that advances in learning and information technologies make it possible, as never before, to individualize curricula *while* making sure that individual students' performance matches or exceeds standards. (I'm talking, here, about sophisticated "data warehousing"/"data mining" systems that enable an individual student's performance to be plotted against school-wide, district-wide, statewide, and national standards as well as against that student's own past record. Such systems foster the development of individualized curricula that closely attend to students' academic strengths and weaknesses.)

Then there's the growing importance in American education of what's called "multiple intelligences" theory, which emphasizes that children have different gifts, different inherent abilities, and which stresses the need to recognize these differences when designing curricula and instructional methods. And the multiple-intelligences movement, with its emphasis on adapting educational technique to the ways in which children actually learn, dovetails with another trend—that of applying the lessons of neurological science to instructional methods and even to curriculum itself. MIT professor and popular science writer Steven Pinker, whose books describing how the brain works have been bestsellers, is, like futurist Bruce Sterling, very concerned about our schools' failure to adequately prepare children for life outside the classroom. In a recent *New York Times* op-ed piece, he takes American schools to task not only for teaching the "wrong" subjects (he thinks all students should receive basic instruction in economics and statistics, for example), but for teaching *in the wrong way*—that is, by neglecting to apply what science has learned about human cognition to what goes on in the classroom (Pinker 2003). The connection between neurology and education is one to which I'll return, below.

Finally—and perhaps most important—there's the unstoppable movement toward greater *choice* in American public education: the growing number of magnet schools, charter schools, and other "alternative" (theme-based and specialized) schools that are offering parents real alternatives in how their children will be educated.

What's so interesting about this current, conflicted situation—in which "standardization" vies with "experimentation"—is that there *are* ways of making these competing, seemingly divergent, approaches come together. One of the ironies of this critical juncture is that some "alternative" schools—magnets, charters, and others—whose instructional methods, curricular approaches, and modes of organization are *anything but* "standard" may offer the greatest hope of improving students' performance according to standard measures. Magnets, charters, and other specialized schools—highly attentive to the needs of individual schoolchildren and specific populations—stand, in many ways, at the cutting edge of American public education. Alternative schools' potential to transform American education for the better is being increasingly recognized: in February 2003, for example, the Bill and Melinda Gates Foundation—which is turning into one of the most important "movers and shakers" on the American educational scene—

gave a grant totaling $31 million to fund the startup of 1,000 new alternative schools across the country (Winter 2003).

Not all such schools are successful, of course, and the jury is still out regarding whether, for example, the charter school movement will live up to its proponents' promise to revolutionize learning, but it is clear that the best magnet, charter, and other specialized schools are doing something that too many "traditional" schools are failing to achieve: they're actually preparing their students for the world—including the workworld—outside the school doors while at the same time ensuring that they "measure up" academically.

Future Schooling—*And* the Future School

At this point, you may be asking yourself what any of this has to do with the school buildings—the physical places—in which we educate our children? The short answer is: *plenty.*

I've described a present-day situation that is, at best, confusing, and I've begun outlining a future in which, it seems, the only certain thing is *change.* Given these realities, it's pretty clear that the most important, overriding principle in school design should be *flexibility.* If a learning space is likely to be used *both* for the traditional, "stand and deliver"-type instruction best suited for preparing students for standardized tests *and* for more exploratory forms of learning combining large- and small-group interaction and individual research, then that learning space *must* be flexible in order to succeed in both its purposes. If, as seems certain, new learning, information, and other technologies are going to continue coming "on line"—and if, as also seems certain, these technologies will quickly be adopted by public schools—then it is *absolutely essential* that schools' learning spaces and infrastructure be designed to flexibly accommodate them.

When you look at the future this way—focusing on the inevitability of change and, therefore, on the need to flexibly accommodate it—"futurism" turns out not to be a flight of imaginative fancy but rather a very pragmatic approach, indeed.

Keeping that in mind, let's take a look at some of the other changes that the future is likely to bring to American education. Some changes, of course, are likely to be expansions or extrapolations of current trends: Because educators increasingly recognize that the performing arts are great tools for building leadership capabilities and fostering the kinds of interpersonal dynamics that enhance teamwork and democratic decision-making, schools of the future are likely to contain a greater variety of (technologically sophisticated) performance spaces, or spaces that can easily be adapted for performing-arts purposes. As everyone grows increasingly conscious of the impact of the physical environment on learning, the indoor-air and acoustical environments of school buildings are likely to be of higher and higher quality. As the manifold benefits of environmental/sustainable, or "green," design become clearer, multiple aspects of a school's interior and exterior environments are likely to be shaped with green-design principles (which cover everything from energy efficiency, to recyclable building materials, to indoor environmental quality) in mind. And as concern grows over increasing rates of childhood obesity, the wholesale retooling of school food programs, with an eye toward balanced nutrition, becomes inevitable. When compared with upcoming technology-based changes, however, these sorts of developments appear tame and relatively uncontroversial. We don't have any trouble envisioning them, and, in fact, we welcome them optimistically and with open arms.

We need to keep that openness and optimism handy when looking at some of the technological advances that lie ahead. Some of the developments discussed below, if and when they are proposed and/or implemented, are likely to be highly controversial and are sure to set off heated debates. But because technology continues to develop so rapidly, I think it's high time that those debates begin, so that the technology-based changes that are introduced into public education result from truly democratic decision-making involving American society at large.

If we don't think about these things now, we're *not* being pragmatic; in fact, we run the risk of letting the future determine us, rather than vice versa.

Human/Computer Interactivity

Even as we prepare this book, the media tell us of successful human-brain chip implants that help disabled people by restoring or simulating sensory abilities, enabling them to function better and more completely by supplementing the brain's power with computer power. It's easy to imagine this kind of technology being more widely applied—for instance, in the form of "remedial reading [or math] chips" implanted in the brains of students with certain kinds of learning disabilities. Such an application would, I think, represent a marriage of education and neurological science like that that Steven Pinker proposes. (And—who knows?—such chips might even eventually enable ordinary human beings to communicate "telepathically," merely by thinking and directing their thoughts at others.)

In a similar vein, voice-activated technologies—in which spoken commands generate computer responses—are a reality today, assisting people with disabilities, those who suffer from repetitive stress injuries, and people who must keep their hands free for non-keyboard tasks. (The 2003 Honda Accord automobile features just such a voice-activated, interactive navigation system.) It strikes me that such technologies naturally lend themselves to educational uses, and that, far from merely "responding" to spoken commands, computers—with whom students will communicate wirelessly—may actually play a role in directing the educational process.

For instance, when the full range of personal data on each student is "warehoused" on school and family servers, the computer will "know" enough about the student to respond to questions such as, "What question *should* I have asked?" The answer will, in effect, control the direction the student takes. As this kind of artificial intelligence advances, it's interesting to speculate about the kinds of answers computers might give to philosophical or spiritual questions. Will the home system give the same kinds of answers as those provided by the school computer? How will school systems deal with church-state questions, and how will parental rights be protected? We don't know the answers to these questions. In fact, we don't even know whether they're the *right* questions—but we can predict with some certainty that this kind of high-level human-computer interactivity will set off some heated debates.

Biotechnical and Genetic Technologies

Interactive technologies like those just described may be supplemented by biotechnical and genetic technologies that enhance mental and physical performance. I can certainly envision the day—perhaps not too distant—when genetic blueprints of each student are available to educators (and their computer "assistants") to help them determine students' inherent strengths and weaknesses and to design individualized educational programs on that basis. I can even foresee educational prescriptions—for both mental and physical activity—being regularly updated (perhaps even daily) through ongoing analyses, conducted in school-based labs, of students' blood chemistry. A changing regimen of dietary supplements and drug therapies would be prescribed to modify and control the changes in students' biochemistry and to prepare students for optimum educational experiences (If nutritional programs were individualized, you can just imagine how the cafeteria environment might be altered!)

In such a scenario, computers would be involved not only in prescribing dietary/pharmaceutical regimens but in monitoring each student's well-being and measuring and assessing the progress he or she makes. As information was collected, the computer would make the necessary adjustments to the prescription, and teacher/facilitators would monitor the computer-student interaction and intervene when appropriate. "Guidance counseling" would come to include mental capacity mapping, sense acuity diagnostics, and the monitoring of brain and overall physical development informed by an intimately detailed understanding of the student's genetic makeup.

The facility-related impacts of these trends are likely to be extensive—involving, for example, the expansion of today's nurse's suites into small-scale, comprehensive diagnostic and treatment centers, and the transformation of physical education spaces into banks of individual workstations equipped with smart machines that use genetic and biochemical data to help individual students maximize physical performance.

Let's not underestimate the importance or scope of the changes that will be wrought by advances in biotechnical and genetic-engineering technologies. Futurist Bruce Sterling, who devotes a chapter of *Tomorrow Now* to the coming biotech revolution, writes that "Biotech is by no means tomorrow's only major technology[,] . . . [but] if it survives and flourishes, it will become the most powerful" (Sterling 2002, pp. 5–6). So, in thinking about schools of the future, let's try to think about what a school in which educational and biomedical functions are intertwined might look like.

We're making a mistake if we don't at least try to anticipate such changes. Schools designed 30, 20, or even a dozen years ago didn't anticipate the explosion in social, support, and technical services that are, today, commonplace features of the educational environment (I'm talking about everything from ESL labs, to planning and placement teams (PPTs), to onsite social workers, to IT support). The result? A situation in which such services are squeezed—uncomfortably—into facilities not designed to accommodate them.

Security, Scheduling, and Environment

Security technology is currently being revolutionized by so-called biometric devices, which "read" and store handprint, fingerprint, and retinal patterns—or even scan and remember human faces—and that permit or disallow access based on whether a person's biometric attributes match those in the security database. Inevitably, biometrics will come to be used in school security systems, providing a much higher level of access control than is possible with the card-access and other, similar systems in widespread use today.

These technologies will reinforce the attitude that the school community is a family, supported by the school's safety and security system. All the members of the community will be connected to one another, and, in effect, the community will protect itself. "Bubbles of caring" will invisibly surround school facilities so that security personnel will be alerted instantly when a problem arises. The technology for this kind networkable system—in which security is based on individual alert buttons worn by all staff and students—already exists and has been implemented at some colleges.

That "bubble of caring" will embrace scheduling, as well. It's more than conceivable that the standard school day will become a thing of the past. As learning programs are increasingly individualized, it will become less and less necessary for all students to arrive at and depart from school grounds at the same times each day. With computerized scheduling and navigational systems in place, there would be no reason why school bus routes couldn't be highly individualized, too, with students being picked up from home, delivered to school, and then taken back home or to after-school activities as their individual schedules require. (In fact, such a system could make sure that the efficiency of a fleet of buses is maximized, potentially leading to reductions in the number of buses needed to serve a school's student population.) Moreover, if students were required to wear or carry chips connecting them to the Global Positioning System, their whereabouts could be constantly tracked and monitored. (Another option would be to surgically implant such chips—making it impossible to lose a student or for a student to elude authority—but this sort of procedure would surely be greeted by outright hostility by some members of the public, making its introduction controversial, to say the least!)

In the school building itself, computers will control the interior environment—not just to modulate comfort conditions as necessary, but also to alter aesthetic characteristics of the environment. We can foresee a day when the colors of walls, floors, and ceilings; images projected on walls; and the amount and quality of light in interior spaces are all controlled by computers, which will change the colors, images, and light as changing educational and recreational activities warrant. On a gloomy day, a ray of artificial (though natural-looking) "sunlight" might stream through the atrium skylight; the mood of a dismal winter afternoon might be enlivened through the projection of a lush lawn onto the floor adjacent to a wall showing a virtual waterfall.

And technology is likely to alter the school environment in another way, as well. Throughout the "Schools of the Future" series, we often speak of the trend—in all public school facilities—toward increased after-hours use of the school building by the larger community. Pursuing that trend further, we can envision a time when educational facilities become even more tightly interwoven with the overall governmental and institutional life of the community. As data resources and support services become ever more intertwined (and instantly, virtually accessible), and as land for municipal construction projects becomes ever more costly (and less readily available), a time may come when it makes a great deal of sense to consolidate many or all municipal functions—governmental, recreational, health, and educational—on a single campus.

The School as "Laboratory"

Whether or not any of the particular changes discussed in the preceding sections is ever implemented, it's clear that technology will continue to radically transform the educational experience. And one of the most sweepingly important aspects of this transformation will be that education—at all levels from preschool on—will become increasingly "experimental" and laboratory-like. Not only will students be in increasingly constant virtual communication with electronic resources, but the seamless interplay between computers and their human users will enable an educational approach that is individualized, problem-solving–oriented, and "experimental" in the best sense of the word. This will be true in all schools—but some magnet, charter, and other alternative schools are even now on the cutting edge of this transformation.

No longer will experimentation be confined to the science lab. Instead, a school building's learning spaces will become all-purpose laboratories in which hands-on and virtual experimentation of many different, interdisciplinary sorts can be carried on. Students—employing personal digital assistants (PDAs) that combine MP3, DVD, cellphone, and laptop computer functions in a single device—will communicate with electronic resources containing vast amounts of information. Wall-mounted "smartboards" will replace blackboards/whiteboards in classrooms and other learning spaces, making even the traditional, lecture-style format a much more interactive experience. Through empirical experiments and heuristic thinking, students will continually be testing the truth and viability of their parents' and teachers' assertions and creatively evaluating the workability and wisdom of schools' organizational structures.

Experimentation, of course, is an ongoing, never-ending process. It involves dialog, the back-and-forth of argument and counterargument, the openness and flexibility required to change one's mind and alter one's direction. It involves interaction—and, of course, interactivity is the foundation of a healthy democratic society. Advances in learning and information technologies don't mean very much—they aren't very valuable—unless they support and extend our ability to work together to find solutions to the challenges besetting us. Education doesn't mean very much—isn't very valuable—unless it prepares our children for the life that awaits them outside the school's doors.

And this, finally, is the earmark of the school building of the future: that it not only enables students to learn interactively, but that it actually nurtures the dynamics of creative, positive, solutions-oriented interaction. It does this in all sorts of ways, from incorporating interactive technological resources into every dimension of learning; to articulating space in ways that enhance human-computer, one-on-one, small-group, and large-group interaction and democratic decision-making; to ensuring that the environment enhances rather than impedes learning.

Does all this sound scary? Well, change always is at least a little scary, and designing facilities to flexibly accommodate change while ensuring that change is for the better is scarily daunting.

But let's not be frightened. To respond effectively to the changes the future may bring, we must ourselves be willing to change our thinking, our strategies, and our priorities. This is a potentially endless task, and one that we—as designers, educators, parents, and citizens—should welcome. Let us, together, begin thinking about the future *now.*

Introduction

Making Space for Kids: A Vision of the Future Elementary School

The future is now. That doesn't mean, of course, that the future is clearly visible. What it does mean is that, unless we begin, right now, to think about what the future is likely to bring—and unless we base our thinking on today's best forecasts about technological advances, developing social and cultural trends, and probable economic, political, and environmental realties—we'll be unable able to respond to the unpredictable demands the future presents.

This book is intended to acquaint readers with some of those advances, trends, and realities insofar as they are likely to alter the nature of public elementary (including pre-kindergarten) education in America over the next decade and beyond. The questions guiding our research and speculation are simple ones: How can we design a school building today in such a way that it will encourage—not hinder—new approaches to elementary education now being discussed or put in place across the country? How can we make certain that the facility itself will be capable of responding effectively to change? How can we ensure that a new elementary school building will easily accommodate the technologies critical to new educational approaches? How can the building foster a climate in which each student is safe and feels that he or she is cared about? How can the facility itself participate in community-building by serving the educational, recreational, cultural, and even governmental needs of the wider community? And, ultimately, how can decision-makers balance all these benefits against the cost of construction and the need to rally and sustain public support for a new school building?

In Part I of this book, we glance briefly at an older urban elementary school that may soon undergo an addition and renovation to see how dramatically facilities have changed over the past century. We follow that with a detailed examination of some of the forces now shaping *all* public school construction—for good and ill. Then, we look at some exemplary "elementary schools of today" whose design addresses several of the major issues—safety and security, parity of educational resources, community building, renovation of older buildings, and so on that are affecting elementary school design at the beginning of the 21st century.

Part II focuses on collaboration—the key to successful planning, design, and project management. The centerpiece of the book, Part III is an exploration of the elementary school of the future, including a discussion of general principles guiding design, specification guidelines, and a series of conceptual diagrams and visual tools. This is followed, in Part IV, by a detailed look at some of the many issues (political, financial, practical, aesthetic, environmental, construction-related, and so on) that now influence—and that will continue to influence—the creation of elementary school buildings.

But, first, let us turn our attention to the overarching question: How do we go about envisioning the elementary school of the future? In the remainder of this introduction, we focus on three critical themes that will guide the conception of elementary school design for years to come:

- The individualization of education and the celebration of diversity
- The socialization of students as democratic problem-solvers
- The use of elementary school buildings by the wider community

There is, as we've already begun to indicate, a very wide range of other issues impacting the design of the elementary school of the future—issues like security and safety, flexibility for changing educational philosophies and for the accommodation of future educational technologies, indoor air quality and other environmental health issues, ergonomics, sustainable design, construction-related issues (cost, feasibility, durability), parity of educational resources and opportunity, and so on. We deal in detail with these and with many other topics over the course of this book. But, to begin with, let's examine the major conceptual forces compelling change in elementary school design.

Individualizing Attention/Celebrating Diversity

In the elementary school of the past, homogeneity was the rule. With only minor variation, students were expected to climb the ladder from the lower to the higher grades in lockstep. They learned more or less the same curriculum at more or less the same time, and whole classes were herded through the same sets of activities from day to day, month to month, year to year. Granted, differences among students were to some extent acknowledged, but these distinctions were drawn with a very broad brush: "accelerated" or "enriched" classes for the "gifted"; "special ed" for the "slow learners" and/or "problem" kids.

This is not to imply that this system of elementary education was totally bad. (It is, after all, the system through which many of today's adult decision-makers traveled, and which many remember with fond nostalgia.) Some teachers were more astute and creative than others, and managed to give their kids as much individual attention as the system permitted. And some students—the "academically inclined," the well-behaved, the able-bodied, those with a stable and secure home life—excelled. Others, however, fared less well, rapidly falling into a pattern of performance that was just good enough to get them promoted from grade to grade. And still others fared disastrously, being "kept back" (with all the shame and social dislocation that entailed) or being awarded "social promotion" that all but guaranteed that they would never catch up with their classmates.

It's been a long and, in many ways, painful lesson, but American society is finally learning that people's differences are something to be celebrated and accommodated, not erased. The era of homogeneity isn't completely over, of course. Debates over the wisdom of social promotion (and its alternative, failure) still rage. And there is one powerful trend—the push to measure and, its proponents hope, improve academic performance through standardized testing—that militates against greater individualization of elementary school education. But, even as classroom teachers around the country protest against having to "teach to the test," there are definite signs that a new educational philosophy—one that emphasizes individualized attention and puts a high value on diversity—is consistently gaining ground. And this new philosophy changes the way that space within the school is conceived, designed, and used.

Multiple Intelligences. First, the theory of "multiple intelligences" put forward in the early 1980s by Harvard University education professor Dr. Howard Gardner has been enormously influential; it now pervades the pedagogy being taught in the nation's teachers' colleges and is dramatically changing the ways in which curricula are being designed. Although the theory is complex and has been extended and refined by Dr. Gardner and his many followers in the years since it was first proposed, the basic premises of multiple-intelligence theory can be put rather simply:

- Children (and the adults they become) have different ways of grasping and *intelligently* interacting with the world around them.
- These different kinds of intelligence can be identified and categorized. (Dr. Gardner has so far described eight distinct kinds of intelligence. A given individual may, of course, demonstrate strength in several of the categories.)
- Our educational system has traditionally focused on developing only two of these kinds of intelligence: what Gardner calls the "linguistic" and the "logical-mathematical" intelligences. It has rewarded those whom it deems verbally and/or mathematically/scientifically talented, while neglecting, ignoring, or actually (though inadvertently) punishing those whose gifts lie elsewhere.
- To be truly effective—to make sure that no one gets left behind because his or her gifts, strengths, and talents don't correspond to a certain lopsided value system—education must address *all* the intelligences.

Pedagogically, multiple-intelligence theory has been especially influential in the development of new instructional styles in which the teacher functions as a facilitator and new ways of designing lessons that depart from the traditional lecture format and that are highly interactive and/or self-directed. This departure from traditional modes has an impact on the ways educational space is conceived and designed—in the classroom and throughout the school. For instance, when a lesson includes a diverse set of activities aimed at developing a diverse set of interests and strengths, classroom space and components (like furniture) must be altered to accommodate that range of activities.

Of course, the kinds of furniture an elementary school classroom contains and the configuration of that furniture have been gradually changing for a long time, with individual students desks being augmented by computer stations, tables for group work, and so on. But the kinds of changes to the classroom that are now being implemented, and those that will be made in years to come, are even more far-reaching. Among these changes are the following:

- *Teacher's workstation.* The old-fashioned teacher's desk was a place to set an apple; the teacher's workstation is a place to set an Apple (or PC!), on which the teacher/facilitator has immediate access to a student's records and a wealth of other resources and from which he or she can control images displayed via a ceiling-mounted monitor or video beam projector. The workstation is designed to facilitate private conferences with students and with parents who visit the school after hours.

- *Personal workspaces for students.* Self-directed learning has made great inroads in the high school curriculum and, in the future, is likely to do so on the elementary level as well. When students pursue projects on their own, they need workspace that's set apart from group activities and reasonably private. It's our expectation that future elementary school classrooms will contain child-size carrels that accommodate a range of different self-directed activities (writing, computer work).

- *Classroom shape and flexibility.* Strict adherence to the traditional rectangular classroom—separated from other (likewise rectangular) classrooms—may itself be softening. To be effective, lessons that emphasize a diversity of individual and small- and large-group activities require a variety of spaces in which those activities can comfortably occur. So, why shouldn't the classroom be configured in an L-shape, or as a crescent or trapezoid? Such shapes might at times be better than the traditional rectangle at allowing several different activities to go on simultaneously in relative visual/acoustical privacy. Moreover, for certain activities, it may make good sense to break down the traditional physical barrier between classes (of the same or even different grade levels). That can be easily accomplished if groups of two or more class-rooms are divided by partitions that can be moved or folded back—creating a single, large space—when desired. And movable partitions *within* a room likewise allow easy, periodic reconfigurations of space to facilitate different kinds of activities. The large point here is that planners and designers need to consider the shape and flexibility of the classroom to ensure that the school's mission is being addressed even at this "elementary" level.

- *Shared resource/gathering spaces.* In fact, why must the bulk of the curriculum in the elementary grades be confined within the four walls of the traditional classroom? Already, certain districts are experimenting with an "agora" or "kiva" concept. (The terms come, respectively, from the ancient Greek marketplace—which was also a marketplace of ideas—and from the community gathering place of Hopi pueblos in the American Southwest.) In this concept, elementary school classrooms are clustered around a central space—the agora or kiva—containing shared resources and providing a generously sized gathering space where groups of students from different classes can meet to pursue projects jointly.

Multiple-intelligence theory is also fostering a renewed emphasis on art and music education in the elementary school curriculum. (Visual/design intelligence and musical intelligence are among the categories identified by

Gardner.) And this new emphasis is leading many districts to insist that new elementary schools contain specialized art and music rooms.

Beyond multiple intelligence theory, neurological investigations into the ways in which children learn are also likely to influence the design of educational space. The goal that will guide educational design in the future is simple to articulate, if more difficult to achieve: to create learning environments that are compatible with the full range of human intelligence and that maximize children's potential by corresponding, in spatial terms, to actual patterns of neurological development.

Differing Needs. Besides fostering children's differing talents, an individualized approach to elementary education recognizes that different kids have different needs. In recent years we've seen the growth of a support system—or, rather, a variety of support systems—intended to meet those needs, and this, too, is having a wide-ranging impact on the way that elementary schools are designed.

The most obvious of the ways in which the recognition of differing needs is changing elementary school design is in the area of special education. "Special education" is an increasingly broad rubric—one whose meaning is continuously being expanded and extended. In Chapter 17, "Exceptional Kids Need More Feet," we use the term loosely to embrace the many kinds of assistance that have been developed to equalize educational opportunity for all children and to try to ensure that no child falls through the cracks—from accessibility requirements for the physically disabled, to programs for the learning disabled, to strategies for dealing with anger and a whole range of emotional, psychological, and social problems. And, in that chapter, we show how all these interventions intensify space demands in new school buildings.

But there are a host of other ways in which attending to children's differing individual needs is influencing how elementary schools work and how they are designed. For example, the traditional school day, ending at about three o'clock in the afternoon, wasn't designed for children whose parents both work outside the home or children of employed single parents. Responding to the problems of "latchkey kids," some districts have instituted what amount to before- and after-school daycare programs. In fact, some districts have taken this response a step further: the Fletcher Thompson–designed Six to Six Early Childhood Magnet School, in Bridgeport, Connecticut, is a full-scale architectural makeover of an existing school specifically conceived to accommodate the strained schedules of working-parent families.

Children's differing medical needs are also being focused on much more strictly and comprehensively than in the past. Gone are the days when the school nurse did little more than apply first aid to scratches and scrapes, dispense the occasional aspirin tablet, and take a feverish child's temperature, sending him or her home if warranted. We're now seeing nurse's suites that are equipped to access any student's medical history and that are stocked with a wide range of pharmaceuticals administered, per doctors' instructions, on a regular basis to certain children (e.g., diabetic kids, hyperactive kids, children with asthma) or available to be used in case of emergency. As the function of the school nurse becomes more complex, the need for onsite medical space increases.

Regarding children's health, among the most worrisome trends in recent years have been a rise in food-related allergies (especially nut allergies) among elementary-school-age children, and a concomitant increase in the severity of reactions of children allergic to peanuts and other foods. While experts debate the reasons behind this, it falls on parents and schools to control allergic children's environments so that they are not made ill by contact with ordinary—but to them very dangerous—substances. Already, many schools have instituted strictly enforced protocols regarding how kitchens and cafeterias are run; the ultimate impact of this trend on the design of food service facilities remains unclear.

Finally, a great deal more attention is being paid to the ways in which children differ ethnically and linguistically. Today, it isn't at all unusual for a public elementary school—even in a suburban district—to have a student population that mixes kids from scores of ethnic backgrounds, who speak dozens of different languages at home. Those long-lived controversies over the wisdom and efficacy of bilingual (usually meaning Spanish/English) education begin to seem quaint nowadays, when a typical elementary school might have students whose first languages are Urdu, Fujianese, Portuguese, Tagalog, Kréyol, Bengali, Arabic, etc., etc. Districts have responded to this veritable Babel by inaugurating a range of academic programs (ESL, remedial programs) and social services that help children and, in some cases, their families adapt. These programs and services, too, require space.

There are, in short, all sorts of ways in which kids are "scooting out" from under—escaping the control of—yesterday's homogenous approach to elementary school education. The situation with which educators must deal grows continually more heterogeneous: with more and more children arriving at their first day of school with fairly well-developed, but differing, abilities (basic computer knowledge, basic reading skills, etc.); with increasing ethnic/linguistic diversity in the school-age population; and with the ever-greater awareness of children's differing intelligences and varying physical, medical, emotional, and social needs.

Accommodating differences and celebrating diversity are—no surprise—expensive propositions. We estimate that up to 25 percent of the space in the typical elementary school being designed and built today is earmarked for special programmatic and support uses—in some cases, uses that weren't even envisioned as recently as two or three decades ago. The list of such special spaces is a long one, and includes (on the academic side) such things as music and art rooms, world language classrooms (sometimes with fiber-optic hookups to the language lab in a district high school), science labs (not unknown in today's elementary schools), special (and specially equipped) facilities for "gifted" programs, and (on the support side) expanded nurse's suites, planning and placement team (PPT) conference suites, family resource rooms, "time out" rooms, after-school daycare facilities, and so on. Not only is this list incomplete, but it doesn't count any of the space that may be added to many areas of a school building to ensure accessibility by physically disabled students.

The desire to foster diversity and diverse skills even extends into the arena of physical education and athletics and affects both indoor and outdoor space. Elementary school gyms are getting bigger, in part to accommodate fitness/agility programs like Project Adventure, which teach a variety of skills (climbing, hazard crossing) that require specialized equipment and hence more space. The craze for children's soccer, which shows no sign of abating, has led to the creation of some elementary school gyms large enough to allow regulation soccer to be played indoors.

Outdoors, blacktopped recess areas have long since given way to elaborate playscapes (for unstructured play) and, in some communities, regulation-size playing fields for a variety of sports. Let's face it. Ours is a competitive society. We want our children to become good at the activities they take up. But becoming good at a sport—soccer, lacrosse, baseball, field hockey—requires practice on a regulation-size field. (We deal with the full range of issues affecting site design and landscaping in Chapter 11, "Site Design and Landscape Architecture for the Future Elementary School.")

All these trends toward greater attention to individual children's talents and needs are likely to become more pronounced in the future. We at Fletcher Thompson are proud to belong to a society that takes great pains to accommodate difference and to ensure not only that all children have an equal chance but that every child has the opportunity to explore his or her own interests and develop his or her own particular skills. But we also know that this celebration of diversity costs money and can lead to discomfort and frustration on the part of boards of education and building committees, who, given the always-present reality of limited budgets, must make hard choices among many different programmatic alternatives. Our appreciation of the difficulty of that decision-making process is one important reason behind the creation of this book, since we believe that, to make good decisions, stakeholders must be informed about all the factors that impinge on school building design. But we also train our eye on saving money wherever possible—and on cutting costs in a way that doesn't reduce the fullness or richness of public education.

Socialization for a Democratic Society

The flip side of diversity, of course, is unity. In this regard, the basic challenge facing educators is the same challenge that has faced American society—at all levels, in all endeavors—since its founding: how to realize the ideal embodied in the motto "E pluribus unum" ("Out of many, one"). In American democracy, of course, unity does not mean conformity. It means agreement on a basic set of values and procedures that allow us to solve problems together while respecting and making room for a wide divergence of opinion.

The process of instilling those values and teaching those collective problem-solving procedures begins, in a formal way, in the elementary grades. In a sense, the job of doing so becomes a tougher one in a pedagogical climate that emphasizes the talents, strengths, and needs of the individual student. The American public school system is built, in part, on the basic premise that there is a value—a very important value—in children learning *together*, as a *group*. Among the hard questions facing educators—and those who plan and design school facilities—as we move into the future is this: How do we design the curriculum, and the space that supports it, in such a way that we simultaneously foster individual learning *and* the cultivation of democracy? This is no "academic" matter, but one that is essential to maintaining the vitality of our way of life.

Paradoxically, some of the measures being introduced to foster individual learning also work to promote group feeling, reciprocity, and socialization. In the previous section, we mentioned the importance of small- and large-group activities in innovative lesson design. While these techniques certainly nurture individual students' strengths, they also develop interactive skills that traditional instructional modes simply ignored. (When the teacher is a lecturer standing in front of a roomful of students, all facing forward and all seated at separate individual desks, little social interaction among students—except the undesirable, disruptive kind!—occurs.) Thus, architectural concepts like the L-shaped classroom, the "kiva," and the flexible classroom whose walls can be pulled back to connect it to other classrooms can all play a part in facilitating the learning of interactive, democratic process.

It's our strong belief that the increasing emphasis in the elementary school curriculum on *performance* is a crucial force in nurturing democracy. Performance is, by its very nature, interactive: student performers learn to become comfortable in front of groups of people—a primary leadership skill—and those who view and listen to a performance learn to appreciate the talents and abilities of the performers. (Preparing for performance is also a strong motivator for children in art, music, and speech programs.)

Performances can also serve as occasions for the whole school community (or large portions of it) to assemble *as a community* to participate, together, in a shared experience. We're therefore very glad to see the return of *auditoriums* (auditoriums, that is, that are large enough to seat the entire student body, at once) to typical elementary schools. For decades, many districts

chose money-saving alternatives to the purpose-built auditorium—
"cafetoriums," "gymatoriums"—that haven't in fact, worked very well.
We're all for flexibility of design, but when a cafeteria or gym is forced to do
double-duty as community gathering space, the opportunities for assemblies
and performances are limited. Operational issues are also much more complex
because of the need for different kinds of furniture for the room's differing
uses; in many cases, the money that's saved in first costs is paid back later
in additional staff and other ongoing operational costs. (And this is not to
mention the fact that such spaces don't necessarily lend themselves, either
acoustically or in terms of stagecraft, to performance purposes.)

We envision a future elementary school in which the spaces proliferate in
which groups of children—groups of different sizes, drawn from the same or
different grade levels—can gather for interactive learning experiences. Some
of these spaces, like the agoras/kivas being introduced in some schools today, will be immediately, directly accessible from the classroom clusters that
surround them. Other such spaces—for instance, a group-inquiry space in
the school's media center, smaller and/or more specialized performance/as-
sembly spaces adjacent to the main auditorium—may form part of the
building's core, or hub.

Communication is a powerful force for promoting unity, and advanced communications technologies—for instance, distance-learning
technologies—will also surely play an increasingly important role in the in-
culcation of democratic values and process in tomorrow's elementary
schools. And who knows whether electronics might not even play a part in
acquainting young children with that most basic of democratic institutions—the vote? We can imagine a time in the not-too-distant future when
students, even comparatively young students, learn about "government by
the people" by regularly expressing their preferences on a whole range of
issues through an electronic polling system.

Community Building

Yesterday's elementary school was a world unto itself, in most ways funda
mentally disconnected from the community that sent its children there. There
were, to be sure, occasions on which the larger community (especially parents) was "invited in"—PTA events, Parents' Days, the school play, a yearly
or seasonal school festival, and so on—but these occasions were infrequent
and highly structured interruptions of the normal routine. The school's participation in the civic life of the wider community was likewise limited: a
lobby might be used as a polling place on Election Day; a gym or cafeteria
might be called into service as a temporary shelter during a local emergency.
But, for the most part, the elementary school building served the school
community only, and it sat empty and unused during hours, days, and
months when school was not in session.

But a public school is not only a community building in the sense that it belongs to the community in which it stands and which, to a greater or lesser

degree, has paid for its construction. A public school can also be *community-building* in the sense of bringing the wider community together. For a relatively long time, communities have realized that high schools can serve this purpose and have insisted that new high schools be designed to accommodate community uses ranging from hosting town meetings, to providing classroom space for continuing education programs, to serving as venues for performance by local theater groups and the athletic events of local sports teams, and so on. It's been much more recently, however, that we've witnessed a widespread recognition that, if properly designed, elementary school buildings can be community-builders, too.

There are, needless to say, a host of design challenges that accompany this trend toward opening the school building to use by the wider community—challenges that involve everything from onsite parking, to outdoor lighting and electric power needs, to the need to segregate (for security reasons) common, or core, areas used by community groups from off-limits academic areas. And some of these challenges are a little thornier in the case of elementary schools than in that of high schools. For example, in areas that are shared by the school and community, how should furniture, toilet facilities, and other components be sized? For children or for the adults who use them after-hours? None of these challenges is, however, insurmountable. As the trend toward inviting the wider community into the elementary school continues to gather steam—as we believe it will—solutions that are tailored to communities' specific needs will be found for all of them.

In emphasizing community use, we do not forget that the primary responsibility of those who participate in the planning and design of the elementary school of the future *is to the students who will learn there*. Architectural and engineering elements have a great bearing on students' safety, comfort, and sense of well-being. For example, a decision to maximize the use of low-maintenance, durable building materials will not only save a district money in the long run by reducing maintenance expenses, it will also foster an environment in which students take pride. (And experience clearly shows that damage begets damage, and that clean, well-maintained school environments tend to stay that way.) Quality lighting systems that don't create glare or interfere with computer screens, ample natural light, facility-wide air conditioning that supports year-round activity—these and other elements all facilitate learning and demonstrate a community's investment in its children's lives and in their future.

But by "commitment to students" we also mean a commitment to *overall design excellence*. We realize, of course, that the real world can be a tough place—one in which genuinely future-oriented visions can be pared down or simply set aside when visionaries come up against the hard realities of budgets, referenda, bureaucratic intransigence and red tape, and simple human inertia and resistance to change. Compromises will always and everywhere be made. But it's our belief—strengthened by Fletcher Thompson's decades of experience of designing schools in New England and the Northeast—that design excellence and futuristic vision can survive the rough-and-tumble processes by which new schools actually come into being. To repeat: There's a much better chance of that happening when stakeholders are well-informed about *all* the factors impinging on school design, when they understand the consequences of their decisions, and when they work collaboratively. Hence this book.

Part I: Yesterday and Today

Chapter 1

Yesterday's versus Today's Elementary School: A Comparative Case Study

Jennings Elementary School in New London, Connecticut, has been in operation for more than 75 years, and, although it's somewhat older than most schools being renovated or replaced today, it provides a telling example of yesteryear's inadequacies. To illustrate the differences, we summarize what exists in the old school and compare that with what the new school—currently under design—will include.

New London is a city in southeastern Connecticut that has its share of urban problems, including a sizable number of disadvantaged families and the municipal government's ongoing struggles to keep property taxes low and the city's facility infrastructure in repair. The new 500-student replacement school will be built alongside the existing 400-student school, which will be demolished when the new facility is completed.

Classrooms
Classrooms in the existing school building range in size and configuration, but it is not hard to find ones as small as 500 square feet—and many of these are being used for the primary grades.

The new specs call for 900-square-foot classrooms, with the following improvements:

- Up to six computers per classroom
- Printers and other technology, including a telephone, a TV monitor, a projection screen, and VCR/DVD equipment
- An abundance of electrical outlets and computer drops
- A sophisticated teacher's workstation centered around a powerful computer, complete with scanner, ceiling projector, and printer
- Sound system
- Lockable supply closets
- Dry erasable boards
- Tack boards
- Bookshelves
- Room-darkening window treatments
- Sinks

Classrooms for Jennings' early-childhood classrooms will have tiled floors with carpeted areas. Each room will have its own unisex toilet facility for students, as well as a "changing" counter. There will be two pre-kindergarten classrooms and three kindergarten classrooms. The classrooms will be accessible from the outside via individual entrances.

Use of these rooms will be flexible, allowing each teacher to establish learning centers and to teach from any section within the room. These students will eat in a separate area, away from older students, in the cafeteria. Storage space will provide room for instructional materials, cots for naps, and play/activity equipment such as large balls, tricycles, and other toys.

Media Center/Computer Room

The existing media center space at Jennings is approximately 1,200 square feet, including stacks, a reading-table area, and a check-out station.

The new media center will double that size, be naturally daylit, and include a full complement of technology. It also will be centrally located in the heart of the building. One section of the library will be carpeted so children can comfortably read books while sitting on the floor. A tiered, carpeted section in this area will allow children to sit and listen to stories being read aloud. A second section of the library will have a storage area accessible to students and teachers and a professional section where teachers can access professional books, journals, tapes, CDs, and the like. This media center will be adjacent to the computer lab.

Special Education Classrooms

The original Jennings School was not designed with special education in mind, and, over the years various nooks, crannies, and closets were adapted to meet special education needs.

The new school will have five special education classrooms, specified as follows:

- Three special education rooms will be "resource rooms" located in proximity to the grade levels they serve. Each will accommodate up to 18 children. Each room will include a special area, segregated from the rest of the classroom, where the teacher can perform appropriate educational testing.
- Two classrooms, accommodating up to 12 students each, will be designed for emotionally disturbed children.

Time-Out Room

The original Jennings school did not contemplate a special space for momentarily disruptive students. The new specification calls for a time-out room.

Reading Recovery/Literacy/Reading Instruction Classrooms

Four rooms will be used for *reading recovery*, a relatively new form of reading remediation/intervention that utilizes one-on-one instruction as well as group remedial instruction. This room will contain a one-way mirror, speakers, and a separate viewing room with six to eight chairs. Specialists can use the mirror system to observe students incognito, and parents can likewise benefit from being able to secretly watch their children engaged in the learning process.

Music and Art Rooms

Jennings, like most of yesterday's elementary schools, did not have specialized music or art classrooms, relying instead on itinerant music and art teachers who occasionally visited each regular classroom.

The new Jennings will possess two rooms dedicated to the music program. The vocal room will accommodate two full classes (up to 56 children), while the instrumental room will serve up to 20 children. These rooms will have power outlets in the floor, a podium, stackable chairs, storage space for musical instruments, and lateral files for storing musical scores.

The new art room will feature adequate storage, cleanup sinks, a kiln room, and a well-equipped photographic area. An emphasis on displaying students' artwork, both in the room itself and elsewhere in the school, will improve student self-esteem.

Specialists' Spaces

The schools of yesterday did not, in general, employ specialists—and hence had no need for specialists' offices or other, related spaces.

Jennings' plans include the following specialists' spaces:

Social Worker's Office. The social worker's office will include appropriate lighting, technology, and one computer as well as a TV, VCR, and phones. Its walls will be acoustically treated. It will also contain enough room for tables, so that the social worker can do group counseling.

School Psychologist's Office. The school psychologist's office will also be acoustically soundproofed so that testing and counseling can proceed in a sensitive, private environment. The office will contain appropriate testing furniture and be easily accessible to all administrative offices. A small conference table with chairs for group work will also be included.

Guidance Office. This office, located in the same area as the other specialists' offices, will be able to be partitioned to accommodate more than one person. Like the other specialists' offices, the space will be outfitted with a full array of technological equipment.

Nurse's Office. Instead of the closet-size space with a desk chair, curtain, and cot that was typical of yesterday's schools, the nurse's office at the new Jennings will include the following:

- A treatment area with counter space, sink, and refrigerator. The treatment area will have safety glass, so that while the nurse is engaged in administrative tasks in her office she can view children who are waiting or in the infirmary.
- An infirmary with three cots separated by curtains that can be drawn from the ceiling to accommodate students who need to lie down for treatment or rest.
- Phones in both the office and treatment areas.
- A computer station in the office.

The area will also have a handicapped bathroom, including a changing area, and a shower so that students can clean up or be cleaned up and change, if necessary.

Gymnasium

Yesterday's elementary school gym typically consisted of a wood-floored basketball court and little else.

The gymnasium of today, as exemplified by the new Jennings gym, has a floor made of a substance that is easy to maintain yet appropriate for athletic activities. The gymnasium will also include bleachers that can be folded down so that spectators can view activities during after-school events. The gymnasium will be equipped with technology, including a large screen adaptable for use with a TV and six computer terminals for instructional purposes, and will contain adequate storage space for equipment. It will be located in such a way to allow students easy access to an outdoor play area and so that members of the community can enter and leave without having to walk through the rest of the school. This area of the building will have its own bathrooms for the convenience of after-school users. The gym will also have wall padding, a public address system, an electronic scoreboard, retractable backboards, and volleyball stanchions. There will be offices for physical education teachers, each with a computer and videotaping technology.

Auditorium

Many elementary schools of yesterday, like Jennings, did not have separate, purpose-built auditoriums. Presentations and performances were given in an all-purpose room (often the cafeteria).

The new Jennings auditorium includes a stage area with performance-oriented backstage facilities, specialized lighting, and a sound system. The auditorium accommodates 1,000—seating for up to 500 students and 500 parents and other guests. The facility can also be used for music instruction on stage and for large group instruction. It accommodates school-community meetings at which students can learn to participate in school decision-making by voting. In addition, the auditorium will be wired and equipped to accommodate technology such as computers, TV, and a large retractable screen for viewing movies. It will be in close proximity to the cafeteria, with a common area in between so that users can enjoy a "lobby"–type environment if refreshments are served at after-hours community events. Bathrooms will be located in this lobby area. Storage facilities for stage props and design materials are included. The entire facility will be designed to allow children with physical disabilities to participate in all activities, whether viewing or performing.

Cafeteria

Many elementary school cafeterias today are combination cafeteria-auditoriums ("cafetoriums") or cafeteria-gymnasiums ("cafetasiums"). At Jennings the cafeteria will be a cafeteria only and will be utilized for school functions, dinners, and parent and community events. Therefore, the room must have an entrance/exit directly to the outside to assist staff in keeping the building secure. As mentioned above, the cafeteria will be located near the gymnasium so that they can share a common lobby and bathroom facilities.

Principal's Office

This windowed office will include a private toilet, carpeting, and appropriate lighting. The walls will be acoustically treated, and the principal's office will be adjacent to the front office and conference room and in close proximity to the counseling and nurse's areas. The room will include a small conference table with chairs to accommodate six to seven people. The principal's office will be readily accessible by the general public.

Family Resource Center

The new Jennings will have yet another facility that did not exist in yesterday's elementary schools—a family resource center. This room will be located near the reception area, where parents can gather to plan activities. It will also be a place for parents to go when they are volunteering in the school. It will be a large enough space that parents can come to school accompanied by younger, preschool-age children.

Computer Laboratory/Server Room

The computer laboratory, absent from yesterday's schools, will be located adjacent to the media center and will include 28 networked computers with Internet access. The server room will be located next door and will be properly ventilated and air conditioned, with room for expansion.

Science Laboratory

The science lab will include laboratory tables and equipment to meet the requirements of students in grades 4 and 5.

Other Components

Yesterday's schools paid little attention to building security, and high-speed communications and related data collection and storage simply didn't exist. Design of the new Jennings school emphasizes these factors, and also pays special attention to issues such as air quality, acoustics, and lighting quality. Like most new schools, Jennings will be fully air-conditioned.

Chapter 2

Cost, Change, and School Construction

Today, the conflicting realities of new school construction are creating a difficult and many-pronged quandary for educators, government officials, architects, and parents and other taxpayers. On the one hand, school design is changing rapidly. Communities across the country are racing to catch up with advances in learning technology and are coming to grips with the need to build schools that are both larger and more complex than the schools of the past.

On the other hand, however, the design of new public schools is not changing as greatly or as quickly as it should, if we are truly to meet the educational challenges of the future. As it stands, the processes by which new schools are proposed, approved, funded, designed, and built do not easily accommodate the kinds of change that the future demands.

In the midst of these contradictory trends, increases in the cost of new schools have continued to outpace inflation. These seemingly inexorable rises in the price a community must pay for a new school building result from a very large number of factors—some only poorly understood by decision-makers—but communities all too often shortchange their own children and future generations of students by attempting to control cost by restricting or eliminating genuinely innovative, genuinely necessary change.

Under these circumstances, how can decision-makers know which kinds of change are good (and should be promoted and supported) and which are not? Further, what steps can be taken by superintendents, boards of education, building committees, state and local officials, parents, and other community members— in other words, by *all* the stakeholders in a new school construction project to control costs while directing change in ways that truly serve their interests? We believe that, if they want to create school buildings that are truly future-oriented, stakeholders must first acquaint themselves with the wide range of factors creating the current impasse. And we believe, too, that there are a number of actions decision-makers can take to facilitate the kinds of change that will transform their communities' new schools into *schools of the future.*

Factors Driving Change: Technology

New public school buildings—elementary, middle, and high schools—are in some ways very different from schools that were constructed even as recently as a decade ago. On an obvious level, new schools are being designed to accommodate a much greater quantity of educational technology—as well a whole gamut of learning technologies that, a mere ten years ago, were either undreamt of or too expensive for public schools to buy and use.

Paralleling the growth in the amount of technology in schools, we've been witnessing a revolution in the uses to which learning technologies are put. For a long time, computers in classrooms (and elsewhere) in elementary,

John C. Oliveto, PE, and Robert J. Poletto, PE, contributed to this chapter.

middle, and high schools mostly served the purposes of *computer training*—that is, acquainting students with hardware and software and developing their proficiency in computer skills. We can gauge just how much that's changed merely by considering how out-of-date a term like "computer literacy" sounds nowadays, when virtually all students (except, perhaps, some in the earliest elementary grades) possess basic computer know-how.

In other words, the use of technology is no longer just an "add-on" or supplement to the curriculum. Rather, technology-related skills have become essential tools in the learning process *in virtually every part of the curriculum*—as crucial to the acquisition of knowledge and to the development of lifelong learning skills as the ability to read and write.

What's more, we believe that we're still just *beginning* to see the changes that technology will cause—both in the way learning happens and in the kinds of skills that will be taught in the public schools. Lately, some educators have begun to say that we've reached a "plateau" in terms of the creation, adoption, and use of new learning technologies. They're wrong. In fact, continuing evolution of learning (and other) technologies and their application will likely *accelerate,* due to pressures of competition in all industries and ongoing globalization of economies. Education in the use of new technologies (and in their operation, maintenance, etc.) will become an ever more essential part of public school curricula, as will instruction in the critical-thinking skills needed to live and work in a world where massive amounts of information, good and bad, are instantaneously available.

Directly related to this explosion in learning technologies are the greater demands placed on the mechanical and electrical systems that serve today's schools. It may be difficult to remember that, just a few decades ago, schools were relatively simple buildings, when looked at from a technical standpoint. Back then, the typical school had one or two electrical outlets in most classrooms; it was heated by steam (there was no air conditioning); ventilation occurred through windows; and makeup air arrived indoors through a simple process of infiltration. By contrast, today's schools require controlled environments for media centers, computer labs, spaces for servers and other information technology equipment, kitchens, science labs, art rooms, music rooms, auditoriums, and gymnasiums. Year-round schools need to be fully air conditioned. Often, a computerized building management system controls the classroom environment by constantly monitoring and adjusting indoor air quality to meet environmental quality standards. Every new school has a built-in telecommunications infrastructure, and—because electrical needs have grown inexorably—is equipped with a power distribution system that's much more generous and sophisticated than those of the past. These aspects of change bear mentioning, in part, because they have had such a significant impact on the first costs of new schools, a subject to which we return at length, below.

Factors Driving Change: The Need for Space

The incorporation of more—and a greater variety of—educational technology is hardly the only way that schools have changed, however. New school buildings are, at every level and in almost every case, *significantly larger* than schools of the past and contain a much greater range of facilities than did their predecessors.

It isn't unusual, for example, for new elementary schools to be purposely designed to accommodate a wide variety of after-hours community functions, playing host to events and groups that range from town hall–type meetings, to senior citizens' activities, to plays produced by community theater companies, to continuing education programs. (This trend toward the "synergistic" off-hours use of school facilities by other community interests is frequently powered by the need for community support of a pending school's funding commitment.)

Other factors—just as important—that are driving the demand for larger and larger schools include:

- *The need for custom-designed spaces for specialized programs.* At the elementary level, these include (for example) specialized classrooms for pre-K education.
- *Demographics.* In many areas of the country, enrollments have been growing and will continue to grow. (In fact, the trend is unlikely to diminish for the next decade or so.) The fact that we have more school-age children means that we need bigger schools (and, of course, more schools) to accommodate them, but demographic changes have another effect on school size. The increasing ethnic/linguistic diversity of our school-age population means, for example, that schools must incorporate space for ESL instruction and for newcomer orientation rooms.
- *Remedial and related programs.* Space demands are also exerted by programs aimed at bringing students up to speed academically (such as "reading recovery" programs), and those aimed at helping students and their families integrate with the school and wider communities (e.g.,"family resources" programs).
- *Accessibility requirements related to the Americans with Disabilities Act (ADA) and other (state and local) legislation and regulations.* Accessibility regulations increase space needs in all sorts of ways. To take just one example: ramps providing wheelchair accessibility to bleachers in a gymnasium might increase the total seating area by as much as 20 percent. Moreover, the ever more widespread desire to provide education for severely disabled youngsters in their home communities (rather than busing them to regional centers) is also adding to local schools' size and complexity. (This topic is discussed in much greater detail in Chapter 17, "Exceptional Kids Need More Feet.")
- *Special education classroom and support space needs.* Relatedly, as more and more students are categorized as having some special education needs, space dedicated to special ed classrooms and support

spaces (including conference rooms where planning and placement teams can meet) grows.

- *The push—sometimes mandated by law—for reduced class sizes.* The arithmetic, here, is simple: reduced class size = more classrooms = larger school facilities.
- *Full-day kindergarten.* The institution of full-day kindergarten programs effectively doubles the amount of kindergarten classroom space needed. (And remember that kindergarten classrooms are generally larger than other elementary school classrooms.)
- *Environmental (especially indoor air quality, or IAQ) requirements.* In some cases, greater concern for the quality of schools' indoor air, as well as the push to fully air-condition schools as the typical school year lengthens, means that more room is needed for mechanical equipment.

And, of course, the learning-technology explosion also pushes space needs upward, not only because of the need for specialized instructional spaces for certain kinds of learning technologies (spaces that are often equipment-intensive and therefore cannot be used for other purposes), but also because of the variety of support spaces that high-tech applications require, such as equipment rooms, offices for IT personnel, and so on. (The too-well-kept secret, which we'll get to a bit later, is that technology can also lead to *reductions* in space needs in some programmatic areas.)

One critical aspect of what can validly be called the "space crisis" has to do with the ratio of gross-to-net square feet. Generally, the ratio of overall square footage (gross) to square footage actually used for programmatic purposes (net) has been growing, in large part because of accessibility requirements and the heightened need for mechanical, electrical, and technological support spaces. Expressed as a fraction, gross-to-net now averages about 1.5 (that is, 3:2). Why is this important? One reason is that state reimbursement levels, which are based on gross square feet per student, have remained static for years. As gross square footage grows in relation to net, a greater proportion of overall construction costs are borne by the local community.

But this growth in the gross-to-net is difficult to control, and efforts to rein it in may not even be to a community's advantage. Many kinds of building enhancements—for example, large atriums that can also serve as gathering spaces for a large portion of the school community—add to gross square footage but also may improve the way a building works. All too often, concern for the bottom line leads building committees to focus on controlling the gross-to-net, eliminating such enhancements. Decision-makers need to proceed cautiously: if architects are handcuffed by the budget, these alternative spaces are not going to happen.

The Construction Cost Upswing

As communities across the country are realizing, *bigger schools are more expensive schools*—a situation made all the more painful by the lack of change in state reimbursement levels. But size—as important as it is—is not alone responsible for the increases in new school design and construction costs. The point must again be made that there are *many* factors driving this trend. Before we turn to those other factors, however, let's take a brief look at some numbers to see just how much costs have risen over the past few decades.

Fletcher-Thompson, Inc. has been designing schools in the New England region for a long time. Our own records indicate that, from 1968 through 1970, new school projects averaged between $26 and $30 per gross square foot. By 1980–1985, typical costs had risen to $60–$65 per square foot. And by 1998–2000 costs were hovering at about $120 per square foot. For projects due to begin construction in 2002–2004, some construction managers are estimating costs at $160 per square foot and higher—meaning that school construction costs will have increased at least 615 percent over the past 30 or so years.(See Figure 2.1.)

To be meaningful, that number has to be compared to the general rate of inflation over the same period. The Consumer Price Index (CPI) tells us that across-the-board inflation since 1968–1970 stands at about 523 percent. So why has inflation in school construction costs been significantly higher than across-the-board inflation as measured by the CPI? There are several reasons:

- *Site development.* Historical data reveal that 30 years ago we were budgeting as little as $10,000–$12,000 per acre for site development on school construction projects. Today, it isn't unusual for those costs to range from $200,000–$250,000 per acre. The reasons behind this enormous jump? In most communities, there are few if any sites that can be used for schools *without* significant remediation and/or preparation

Figure 2.1. Cost History (Dollars per Square Foot)

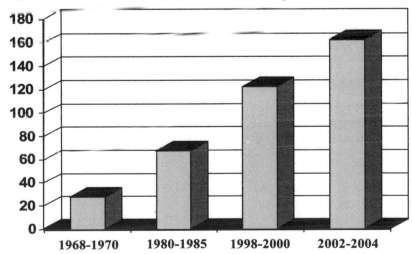

(extensive grading, rock removal, etc.). In most places, there are no more "perfect" sites for the construction of new schools. And paralleling this decline in the number and quality of suitable sites is the growth of regulatory agencies and regulations—regarding wetlands and other environmental issues, traffic patterns, site accessibility, preservation of trees, and so on—that must be satisfied before construction can proceed.

- *Shortages of skilled labor and building materials.* During the super-hot construction market of the mid-1990s through 2000, costs were driven up by materials and labor shortages. Remarkably, the construction sector (especially residential construction) remained strong during the economic downturn of 2001, and shortages of skilled tradespeople and materials were still in evidence. As of this writing, only a few months after the terrible events of September 2001, the situation has become much less clear. On the one hand, America and the rest of the world took an enormous economic hit, and the longer-term depressing effects on the U.S. economy—the construction sector included—are unknown. On the other hand, however, the massive rebuilding effort that will doubtless soon be under way in New York City may, despite a possible national recession, mean that labor and materials shortages will continue to be felt, especially in the Northeast.

Materials and labor fall into what are called the "hard costs" of construction. But the bottom line is also being affected by what are termed "soft costs"—for example, the "escalations" that construction managers (CMs) build into their estimates when trying to predict the ultimate cost of a school that is being planned or designed now but that won't be completed for another three to five years. These escalations are, in effect, hedges against future uncertainty extrapolated from available data. Historically, such estimates have tended to err on the high side, for very good reason. State approval and local referendum processes require that there be an estimated dollar-figure for new school construction; if estimates are too low, a community might have to go back to the state and/or the voters to get more money, which could endanger a project or, at the very least, greatly delay its being built. Even though escalations generally overshoot the mark, it will come as no surprise that communities find ways of spending the difference between the estimated and actual construction cost, which means that these escalations play a real part in pushing up inflation.

This situation of shortages described above has been worsened, over the past few years, by a general (and understandable) reluctance on the part of CMs and contractors to take on public-sector jobs, including public schools, when there has been plenty of high-paying, faster-paying private sector work available. As we indicate above, this may change as the economy declines, but it needs to be mentioned here among the factors that have made new school construction a more problematic enterprise.

Perhaps the best way of characterizing all these factors, grouped together, is *project complexity.* In every conceivable way—from the addition of learning technology, to the imposition of accessibility requirements, to the exigencies of the construction market (and so on and so on)—our public school buildings and the process by which they are planned, designed, and built have become more complex.

Impediments to Change: The Process

Unfortunately, we're stuck with a process for proposing, approving, and funding new schools that does not accommodate this increased complexity very well. We've already indicated that state reimbursement levels have not risen to meet contemporary schools' increased size and complexity. But this is hardly the only way in which the process, as it now functions, impedes change for the better. Here's a brief list of some of the other ways the process raises hurdles to change:

- Onerous deadlines (related to state approvals) that require communities to make decisions too quickly and without sufficient consideration.
- A lack of information, on the part of boards of education and building committees, regarding the real costs/benefits of a wide range of innovative features that are typically rejected because they are seen as too expensive. These kinds of features include (among many others) air-conditioning for the entire school; soundproof, easily operable room dividers to allow flexibility in classroom size; ceiling-mounted, computer-friendly projection screens in each classroom; ergonomic furniture; "zoned" electronic security systems.
- A foreshortened educational specifications process, in which a (perhaps innovative) mission statement is adopted but then forgotten, because there isn't the time or knowledge to work out how that mission can be furthered by truly future-oriented design.
- A referendum process that rewards a traditional, conservative approach.
- A tendency for political concerns to overpower educational needs.

Impediments to Change: Traditional Attitudes

Everyone fondly remembers how things were "back then"—when he or she was in school. In many ways, that nostalgia is a good thing, since it provides a emotional link between adult decision-makers and our public schools. But it can also foster a conservatism that resists change. On the most obvious level, this traditionalism strongly influences how school buildings look. People rightly feel that a school building "should look like a school building," and architects agree. But there is a world of difference between an attitude that insists that new school buildings rigidly copy past architectural styles and one that allows architects to explore ways of acknowledging tradition while creating designs that are also genuinely new.

That traditionalism on the part of the public at large is paralleled by a conservatism among some educators and other school personnel who, used to doing things in certain ways, are also resistant to change. One sees this, for example, among certain librarians who refuse to acknowledge that media cen-

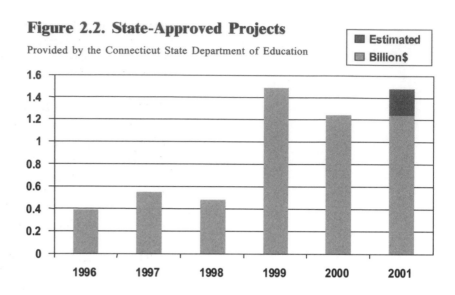

Figure 2.2. State-Approved Projects

Provided by the Connecticut State Department of Education

Legend: ■ Estimated ■ Billion$

ters are now *in transition* and in the future are likely to need much less shelf space for housing paper-and-ink books. Certainly it's true that printed books aren't going to disappear—or not for a long time to come—but it's equally true that, as more and more resources are available electronically, the need for stack space declines. To serve the future, this transition should move forward more quickly. As it stands, media centers are in many cases being oversized—being built for yesterday's rather than tomorrow's book-storage needs.

Space—in schools as in all other workplaces—isn't emotionally neutral. Space is also "turf," and resistance to change can also originate in the desire on the part of faculty and departments to defend their territory.

It's worth noting here that impediments to using learning technologies as effectively as possible don't always have to do directly with space—though they may indirectly affect the amount of space needed. For example, in the state of Connecticut, there is no coordination of school-day schedules among districts, which makes it hard to employ distance-learning technologies efficiently. If school-day periods were the same statewide, it would be much easier to schedule real-time distance-learning classes to cross district boundaries, and this would have the twin effect of cutting down on duplication of effort that already exists while expanding the opportunities for employing distance learning.

There's an emotional component, too, to the widespread resistance we see to combining smaller, local schools into larger district-wide facilities. It's widely felt—among educators and the general public—that a number of smaller schools dispersed across a district are psychologically and practically better than a single, centralized facility that serves all of the district's primary, elementary, middle, or high school students. As we discuss in Chap-

ter 3 (in the section relating to the John Trumbull Primary School, in
Watertown, Connecticut), the resistance to this concept is stronger when
applied to the lower grades than to the higher, which makes sense: younger
children have a harder time adjusting to large schools than do older children, and there is valid concern about the hardship and inconvenience that
busing young students for long distances can cause for them and their families. But the large-school concept has met with resistance on the high
school level, as well.

When we say that part of the reluctance to consolidate schools into larger,
regional facilities is "emotional," we do not mean that it is "wrong." As
we've just indicated, there are understandable reasons for opposing such
plans. The problem is that such opposition generally ignores three strong
arguments that can be made in favor of consolidating schools into larger,
district-wide facilities:

- *Large, consolidated facilities permit economies of scale that aren't
  possible if students are dispersed among a number of smaller schools.*
  That is, a large, consolidated school can provide a wealth of
  educational resources (a greater variety of books in a media center, a
  greater variety of enrichment programs and faculty to run them) than is
  possible if education dollars have to be divvied up and distributed
  among a number of schools serving students at a given level.
- *Consolidated facilities reduce inequities between richer and
  poorer areas of a district.* When all students—no matter whether they
  come from higher- or lower-income families or neighborhoods—attend
  the same school, they all receive the same, high-quality education *and*
  they share diverse life experiences and viewpoints.
- *There are proven ways of designing and organizing a large school to
  reduce or eliminate the negative psychological/social effects.* The
  school-within-a-school (or "cluster" or "house") concept has been
  successfully employed in schools ranging from primary to high
  schools. Under this form of organization, a student stays within the
  same cluster, or house, throughout his or her years at the school. That
  provides a feeling of continuity, and the limited size of the cluster
  prevents children from feeling overwhelmed, as they might within a
  very large school not broken down into these smaller units. Architectural design supports the cluster concept by carefully demarcating
  areas that belong to each cluster and those common areas shared by
  the entire school.

Fostering Positive Change: What Can Decision-Makers Do?

This is the hard part, because it not only calls for procedural changes and
careful decision-making on the local level but also demands that all stakeholders press for fundamental changes on the state level. Let's take the
issue of educational specifications development. A good, thorough "ed
spec"—one that will really help educators and designers implement the
goals of a future-oriented mission statement, throughout the curriculum—is

a very rare commodity. Why? Because to develop good ed specs, local boards of education often need expert guidance from consultants and architectural designers, and these kind of services cost money that is very hard to come by during the planning stage. Boards of education, already financially squeezed, can seldom find money in their budgets to pay for adequate planning, and state departments of education provide no resources for this critical, up-front phase of the planning process.

What can be done? Well, on the local level, it may be incumbent on municipal legislators (town councils, etc.) to include such funds in their education budgets for years when a new school planning process is scheduled to begin. On the state level, three measures (at least) are sorely needed:

- State legislatures must be pushed to change the law regarding reimbursements, making money available to departments of education to distribute to local school districts *in advance of project submittals,* to assist them in developing ed specs;
- State departments of education must update their criteria for space use within the modern school facility and guide the evolution of school facilities by stipulating *proper* guidelines for funding and approval; and
- State D.O.E.s must be encouraged to develop a range of other resources to help individual districts plan new schools. These non-financial resources might include such things as comparative data on school buildings recently completed or now under design/construction around the state, sample educational specifications (for elementary, middle, high, and magnet schools), and a list of consultants offering help in developing ed specs.

It is, quite frankly, astonishing to us that such resources do not now exist in the state of Connecticut—which spent half a billion dollars on new school construction during 2000 (and not a single dollar on pre-submission planning!)

What else can local decision-makers do? As they plan a new school, they can focus on ways in which technology can help them control the size of the facility and thereby control costs. In this chapter, we've already suggested one area (stack space in media centers) in which creative thinking about the use of technology could help lessen the demand for space. And there are other ways—of even wider scope—in which the technologies that are already altering the learning process can also be used to cut the size, and therefore the cost, of the school of the future.

For example, the expansion of individualized programs of study utilizing online learning means that much classwork can be done away from the school building itself—and that there's no longer any real reason that *all* students must attend school during the same hours each school day. Instituting staggered or flexible schedules would reduce the number of classrooms and other learning spaces needed at any given time. Staggered/ flexible schedules would likewise reduce the size of school bus fleets, since buses would be operating throughout the day. (Current communications and navigational technologies could allow drivers to change routes as students' schedules change.) A smaller fleet would mean that school bus staging areas could also be reduced in size.

Utilizing (fully air conditioned!) school buildings year-round could likewise reduce overall space needs, especially if a trimester-type schedule were implemented in which each student would attend school for two of the three trimesters each year (meaning that only two-thirds of the total student body would be in school at any given time).

Are such ideas "radical?" They may at first seem so. But the fact is that communities across the nation are already making fundamental changes to the school day and school year—and that our school buildings are already becoming 24/7/365 facilities (or nearly so). What we're proposing is that this process of change be consciously coordinated with new-school planning and design. That's one way to discover how change can work for us—reducing the size of new schools, controlling the cost of school construction, and modifying school design in ways that truly serve educational methodologies of the present and the future. (See Figure 2.2.)

Chapter 3

**The Elementary School of Today:
Four Exemplary Projects**

In an important sense, there is no such thing as "the" elementary school of today. True, architects and educators are coming to share a core philosophy of elementary education—some of whose central themes are developed in the introduction to this book—and a generalized set of principles guiding elementary school design continues to evolve. Still, every school planning and design process must respond to a large number of particularities. These might include—to choose just a few examples—budget limitations, site constraints, the size and demographics of the student population, the degree and kind of community use the building will house, and/or the specific educational vision the school is intended to embody and foster. As we emphasize throughout this book, every school construction project is unique—or should be—and there is, therefore, no single model for a successful elementary school design.

This chapter presents four elementary school projects—two recently built, one slated for construction in the near future, and one now under design development—that we believe to be exemplary. In important respects, they are very different from one another. In each case, the school's designers were charged with responding to a distinct set of issues—a district-wide consolidation, a city's effort to creating smaller school environments, the desire to preserve an existing structure while creating spaces suitable to today's educational approaches, and so on—and, hence, were called upon to create distinctive solutions that met each particular community's needs. Despite—or because of—these differing emphases, the schools are, we believe, equally successful.

Project #1
John Trumbull Primary School
Watertown, Connecticut
Grades pre-K through 2
Designer: Fletcher-Thompson, Inc.
Completed: 2000

by Patricia A. Myler, AIA

Key issues:
District-wide consolidation
Big school versus little school
Community use
Site limitations
Flexibility

John Trumbull Primary School: Academic Entrance.

John Trumbull Primary School: Reading Room.

A District-wide Consolidation. The Watertown, Connecticut, school district's decision to consolidate all its pre-kindergarten and K-2 classes in a single facility (housing nearly a thousand students) grew from two motives. The Board of Education and superintendent were philosophically invested in creating an environment in which new educational concepts—team teaching, cross-grade instruction, and interactive, high-tech learning—could flourish in the critical early elementary grades. Consolidation would allow resources to be combined and shared, enabling a much richer concentration of resources (faculty, specialized learning spaces, educational technology) than would have been possible if resources had to be divvied up or duplicated among a number of schools.

But the idea of creating a new facility for the entire district—one with spacious, generously outfitted, and technologically up-to-date classrooms and common spaces—also had a practical political dimension, that of correcting a perception of unequal distribution of educational resources between the district's two diverse areas. Indeed, the project's concern for parity was key to developing community support leading to the passage of the school bond referendum making the new John Trumbull Primary School possible.

Big School versus Little School. Bringing together so many very young schoolchildren in one building—the design population was 980—produced a significant conceptual challenge for the project's architects. Typically, K-5 elementary schools are designed for populations of no more than 300. Given that the experience of going off to school is often a bewildering one for young children, how could a building more than three times as large as a typical elementary school be designed in such a way that schoolchildren would not be overwhelmed?

The solution is a "school-within-a-school" (house or cluster) concept that gives children a manageable, coherent environment and—because children remain in the same house as they progress from one grade to the next—provides continuity through the early school years. Coherence and continuity are reinforced through a bold, easily comprehensible wayfinding scheme that identifies each cluster with a specific primary color and geometric shape-yellow circles, blue squares, green triangles. All the colors and shapes are brought together in common areas such as the cafeteria, media center, and gym.

Community Use. Like many other elementary schools nowadays, the John Trumbull Primary School was intended for heavy after-hours use by community and civic groups. Here, the design challenge involved segregating common areas, which would also be used by the public, from strictly academic areas in order to maintain security while fostering ease of access for schoolchildren and adult users alike.

The "public" and "academic" sides have separate entrances for students and community users. A "main street" links the academic clusters with the

John Trumbull Primary School: Pre-K Gross Motor Skills Area.

John Trumbull Primary School: Canopy Entrance.

John Trumbull Primary School: Media Center.

shared areas. Academic spaces are child-scaled; the public side mixes child- and adult-scaled components, including a full-size basketball court in the gymnasium. The stage, which is between the cafeteria and gym and can open onto either room, is outfitted with technical capabilities that are more sophisticated than is usual for primary schools.

Security is also enhanced by segregating vehicular traffic into distinct streams for parent drop-off, school buses, and service/delivery. The main administration office is strategically located to view the main door. Placing the bus queuing area at the entrance to the academic area lets students move directly from buses to a canopied entryway. Outdoor play areas are cradled within courtyards on either side of the school's "main street."

Site Limitations. The site's limited size created its own challenge: how could the needed density be achieved while ensuring that all students would have grade-level access/egress from every area, as state law requires for children in the early elementary grades? (In other words, the building could not be two stories high if that meant that any children would have to ascend or descend stairs to get in or out of the building.) The solution—like the challenge—was provided by the site. Because it slopes steeply, the needed second level could be situated below the main level on the academic side of the building while still permitting grade-level access from anywhere in the school.

Flexibility. The building flexibly accommodates change. Additional power and data drops can easily be added to classrooms (each now equipped with five computer stations at the perimeter) if and when computers are installed at individual desks. Should computers be fully integrated into classrooms, the two computer labs (adjacent to the media center) can easily be converted to media-center space. Large pocket doors between paired classrooms can be opened for team teaching. Gypsum wallboard construction permits easy demolition of walls to create larger classrooms, if needed.

Sometimes several factors combine to produce a design decision, and that was the case at the John Trumbull Primary School. For example, one small though important question involved how to size fixtures in lavatories—for child or adult users? Ultimately, the decision was made to specify standard, adult size fixtures—except in the pre-K area. There were three rationales: (1) after-hours adult users would require standard-size fixtures; (2) children would be comfortable with these, since they are used to using them at home; and (3) specifying standard-size fixtures would increase the building's future flexibility, since any eventual conversion of the building to serve older students would not require re-equipping the lavatories. That last reason is especially important, since changes in the district's school-age population are to some extent unpredictable, meaning that, at some point in the future, the building might have to be converted to serve a wider grade range. This kind of long-term flexibility is also a critical element in elementary school design today.

Project #2
Chicago Public School
Chicago, Illinois
Grades pre-K through 8
Designer: Marble Fairbanks Architects
Scheduled for completion 2005

by Karen Fairbanks and Scott Marble

Key issues:
Urban schools
"Bootstrapping"
School/community/landscape continuities
Generative space
Small-school identity
Flexibility
Sustainability

Chicago Public School: Ramps provide accessibility.

Chicago Public School: Interior Street.

Urban Schools. As in other urban areas, many public schools in Chicago currently operate significantly above the desired capacity for the most effective learning. Because extensive research indicates that children perform better in smaller school environments, large cities have begun experimenting with strategies that organize larger schools into smaller units. This as-yet-unnamed elementary school, which will bring together two existing schools and is scheduled for construction on Chicago's South Side, organizes an 800-student elementary school into four smaller schools that will have some independence but still share common facilities and be under the direction of a single principal. The project was chosen from among four finalists in a Chicago Public Schools Design Competition; it has since been awarded a 2001 P/A (Progressive Architecture) Award from *Architecture* magazine.

"Bootstrapping." A process of growth in which a small amount of energy or input triggers the evolution of a larger system is called *bootstrapping*. Like a computer using the smallest, simplest program to boot itself up, a building can act as a bootstrap for the growth of communities within it, providing simple spatial platforms and links that allow relationships to evolve. In this project, the school building functions as a bootstrap on multiple levels, providing a structure to encourage self generation both within the school and the community. Each classroom provides the platform for the generation of a group dynamic between the students and their teachers and is their link to their small school. The generative space of each small school acts as a bootstrap for the school to generate its own identity and link to the larger community. The parent/teacher rooms and classrooms that bridge across the interior street link the small schools, providing a shift in scale from the small school to the larger one. The interior street is a bootstrap to the community.

School/Community/Landscape Continuities. The school, community, and landscape are continuous in multiple ways. Continuities within the school are defined by its circulation weave, the three-dimensional intersection of three primary paths of movement: the ramps used within the small schools, the interior street connecting the small schools to the larger community, and an upper level path connecting the small schools and bridging the interior street. The primary movement of students and teachers in the school building is facilitated by a system of ramps that allows all students of varying abilities to access all programs. The ramps allow for a two-story arrangement of programs that facilitate interaction between the small schools, the shared programs, and the community circulation space of the interior street. The school building is compact and efficiently arranged so that travel time is minimized and the identity of the small schools remains clear.

The school's interior street, the main community circulation space of the school, is aligned with West 103rd Place. By continuing the topography of the neighborhood within the school, the building provides a naturally placed, direct link with the community. Community involvement is also increased through the community garden strip along 103rd Street, which

Chicago Public School: Plan of Second Level.

Chicago Public School: Generative Space.

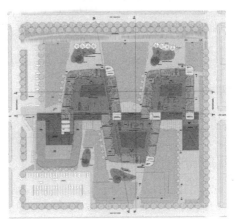

Chicago Public School: Plan of Main Level.

includes community plots, paths, benches, and public art projects. This garden invites the community into the school site and creates a direct link between the busy community along that street and the community of the school. Community use also extends to the other landscape facilities, such as the school gardens, playgrounds, and basketball courts.

The school is also continuous with the landscape, sloping up out of the landscape towards the center of the building, while the grassy play areas slope down towards the interior street. This continuity—which creates complex and varied learning ecologies within a rich topography of spatial, material, and social relationships—is reinforced through the use of grass on the classroom roofs. The landscape of the site interweaves large, soft grass areas and hard surfaces to play on with interspersed islands of resilient playground surfaces, plantings, and "exploration gardens" of water, sand, and wind.

Continuities between inside and outside are also essential to the school's design. Each shared program has an adjacent outdoor space to invite learning and experimentation in and out of the actual classroom. The outdoor spaces are accessed directly from each space and are clearly visible from inside. The art room, science lab, music room, assistive technology training, and discovery center all have exterior garden courts. The surface material of these outdoor courts slips into the interior street, creating a tactile connection between the spaces. The library, dining, therapy center, and K/pre-K discovery center open to the exterior courtyards located within the building, each landscaped with distinct material surfaces and plantings.

Generative Spaces/School Identity. One important aspect of small-school philosophy is that each school should have its own identity and community, with a shared vision and goals. This school facilitates the formation of identity and community by providing spaces where members of the school community can gather and interact to generate the vision, spirit, and direction of that school. Each small school has one large generative space at the top of its ramping classrooms, overlooking both the interior street and the outdoor courtyards. This flexible space allows each school to define and configure it according to its own needs, and the generative spaces will develop their own character as the small schools establish their vision.

The generative space, the courtyard adjacent to it, and the outdoor play space of each school provide the spatial platform for each small school's identity to evolve. Each outdoor play space has a distinct element that identifies the school: a butterfly garden, wind sculpture, water exploration pool, or a sand play area. The courtyard in the center of each school brings light to the circulation space and links that school to the program adjacent to it. Each courtyard is landscaped to relate to the activity of the program next to it and to provide each school with a different exterior focus. Together, these three communal spaces provide a generative framework for the creation of a school identity and spirit. As children spend a number of years in their small

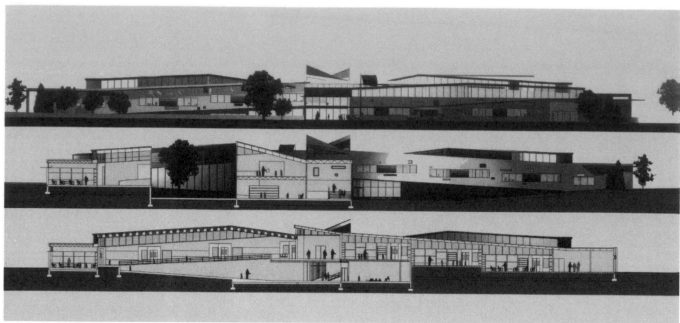

Chicago Public School: Elevations.

Chicago Public School: Model.

school, moving from room to room, their relationships to the generative space, the courtyard, and the landscape become rich and layered with experience.

Flexibility. The school building is designed to be able to expand into the site or to shift the configuration of classes between small schools. Classrooms may be added to each small school, accommodating population growth. The bootstrap connections over the interior street also allow for expansion and contraction of each small school within the building. These connections can accommodate extra classrooms and can also allow the boundaries between the separate schools to shift or, if desired, to disappear altogether. The generative spaces provide flexibility for each school to reconfigure or readjust their space to accommodate changes in curriculum, teaching methodologies, and student needs. The classrooms are designed to address the different teaching styles and needs of each teacher. Storage and surface areas are maximized and are able to be configured in a variety of ways, allowing for individual workspaces, small-group workspaces, whole class meetings, project space, and teacher alcoves.

Sustainability. Sustainable design is equally concerned with life-cycle cost and environmental awareness. The first criterion establishes feasibility and economic sustainability over the long haul; the second is educational, allowing each student to perceive his or her place in the natural order established by the sun, the winds, and the design of the building and its integral landscape.

Building-wide systems choices establish life-cycle sustainability. A simple, highly insulated structure with relatively high mass permits passive heating and cooling effects. Community return on fixed capital is maximized by a building design that promotes multiple uses year 'round. All classrooms

Chicago Public School: Rendering.

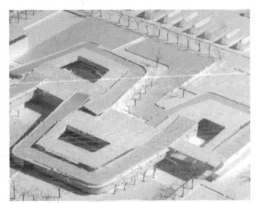

Chicago Public School: Model.

have gently sloping, planted roofs that, although they are more expensive to install than conventional roofs, are longer lasting, easier to maintain, and more reliable and highly insulating over the long term. These planted (or "green") roofs will also retard storm runoff and serve as a pre-filter for graywater and irrigation systems. Photovoltaic skylights over each school's common areas will provide appropriately shaded daylight and generate power for the school's most socially generative activities.

A natural awareness of the indoor environment is the final object of all sustainable design. Classrooms are naturally daylit with light shelves sometimes doubling as shades against direct sunlight. The school rooms are designed for cross-ventilation to minimize energy costs in comfortable spring and fall weather. Material selection for the classrooms will be subject to a rigorous procedure to specify benign, durable local materials, many from recycled stock, with low embodied energy levels and no off-gassing after building commissioning.

Each school is given its specific identity, in part, by its architectural response to solar orientation. North elevations are more closed, and protected by landscaped windbreaks. In the courtyards, canopies shade against the hot summer sun but welcome warm winter sunlight. In the playgrounds, the landscaping provides sheltered microclimates, extending outdoor play into the late fall and permitting it to start again early in the spring. Many design features will decrease energy and maintenance costs while increasing the environmental awareness of the students, making the building itself an object lesson in sustainability.

Additional project credits:
Consulting engineers: Ove Arup & Partners
Sustainable design: Kiss and Cathcart Architecture

Project #3
Southwest Elementary School
Torrington, Connecticut
Grades pre-K through 5
Designer: Fletcher-Thompson, Inc.
Completed: September 2001

by: Julie A. Kim, AIA, and Daniel Davis, AIA

Key Issues:
Addition to and renovation of existing building
Community context
Natural daylighting

Southwest Elementary School: Renovated Building (l.) and Addition (r.)

Southwest Elementary School: Addition, with Bay Windows and Clerestory.

Addition/Renovation. The Torrington, Connecticut school district, with the strong support of Mayor Mary Jane Gryniuk, was determined from the start to preserve as much as possible of the original 1904 building in the renovation of Southwest Elementary School. This immediately posed a number of challenges for the design team. The building had originally been handsome, featuring quality materials like brick walls and wood floors, and many community members felt a strong emotional attachment to it, having attended elementary school there themselves. The building had deteriorated over years of neglect, however, and in many ways the early 20th century structure was unsuited to today's elementary school curriculum.

The ground floor was sunk below grade level and entrances were between the ground and first floors, thus requiring stairs at each entry point and limiting access to the building by disabled students. Insufficient space for general classrooms on the first and second floors forced the school to use corridor space for educational purposes, setting up partitions and letting classroom activities spill out into the unusually wide main hallway. Art and music rooms, gymnasium, and cafeteria were all relegated to the poorly lit and cramped ground floor. Lavatory facilities, HVAC systems, and wiring were inadequate throughout.

Designers adopted a two-pronged strategy that enabled them to preserve the best features of the original building while overcoming its limitations through the addition of new, modern spaces. General classrooms remained in the original building, taking advantage of its high ceilings, large windows, and traditional feel. The new scheme somewhat reduced the size of the large, double-loaded central corridor, creating space for lavatories and other support facilities. The ceiling height was maintained in the classrooms but lowered in the corridors, allowing for the addition of necessary wiring, sprinkler pipes, and HVAC-system ductwork. The attractive but worn wood floor was replaced with a new vinyl product that looks like wood plank flooring, thereby preserving the charm of the original, but that is easier to maintain and softer on the feet. Undesirable relics of early 20th century construction, such as lead paint and asbestos, were removed from the site. Thus the renovation of the existing building preserved the classic feel of the traditional classroom spaces while bringing the building up to modern construction standards.

To supplement the original 30,000-square-foot Southwest School, the design team created a one story, 24,000-square-foot addition that runs on an axis perpendicular to and along the back of the original building. This airy addition houses the larger program spaces, including cafeteria, media center, gymnasium, kindergarten classrooms, and administrative offices, thus relieving the overcrowding of the original ground floor. (The revamped ground floor now hosts only art and music classrooms.) The three entrances to the building have been moved to the new addition, where they are on grade level and all open onto one main corridor. Disabled access has been further improved by the addition of an elevator serving all three floors of the original building. Visual continuity has been maintained through the use of

Southwest Elementary School: Natural Light in Interior.

Southwest Elementary School: Renovated Classroom.

Southwest Elementary School: Media Center.

brick and other exterior materials that coordinate well with the original building.

Community Context. Southwest's setting in the midst of a relatively dense residential neighborhood added to the complexity of the addition/renovation project. The existing site was simply too small to accommodate modern facilities, so the city of Torrington decided to purchase eight adjacent properties in order to allow for the building addition and new outdoor play spaces. Unfortunately, this displaced a number of families who had, in some cases, been living on the neighboring properties for generations, causing an outcry amongst the local community. While residents were eventually mollified by a generous compensation package, the Torrington case illustrates the difficulties that can be encountered in renovation and addition projects, especially in densely built urban settings.

Despite this drawback, the renovation enhanced the school's participation in the community in several ways. Modernized gymnasium and media center facilities are more conveniently situated for public use in the new addition, which separates them from general classroom spaces. Improved handicapped accessibility makes these amenities available to all members of the community. Finally, a streamlined parent and bus drop-off scheme and re-designed parking areas have diminished the school's impact on neighborhood traffic circulation patterns.

Natural Daylighting. Perhaps the most striking feature of the renovated Southwest School is the prevalence of natural light. The design team was committed to the benefits of daylighting, citing research that indicates natural light can lead to greater school achievement, improved attendance, and greater attentiveness. Again, the structural advantages of the original building were maximized while more modern design principles were employed in the addition. The original windows were replaced with higher-quality insulated glass while retaining the large window openings. The solution for the new addition included three clusters of clerestory. The center clerestory spine runs the full length of the building from the main entrance to the media center. The two flanking spines run over the cafeteria and the kindergarten rooms. The clerestories are located 16 feet above the floor with the pitched ceiling rising another 10 feet beyond the ribbon windows. In these spaces, natural light streams from overhead, giving a sense of openness and light reminiscent of being in a museum or religious structure. Full-height windows at the ends of the spaces also contribute to a sense of connection with the outdoors. To further enhance the amount of natural light, there are roof areas a few feet below the rows of clerestory which act as a lightshelf. These areas reflect light onto the ceiling, diffuse it, and allow more daylight to penetrate down into the space. Finally, a bold new color scheme throughout the school includes shades of coral in the cafeteria, lime-green and blues in the kindergarten rooms, and bright lemon yellows on the ground floor level, giving each area its own character and sparking students' senses.

Project #4
Trumbull Elementary School
Trumbull, Connecticut
Grades pre-K through 5
Designer: Fletcher-Thompson, Inc.
Scheduled for completion: 2004

by Joseph G. Costa, AIA, and
L. Gerald Dunn, R.A.

Key Issues:
School-as-village
Architecture in the service of the spirit

Trumbull Elementary School: Lobby Concept.

Trumbull Elementary School: Northwest Elevation.

Trumbull Elementary School: Southwest Elevation.

School-as-Village. Residents of the small town of Trumbull, Connecticut wanted their new elementary school to have a "noninstitutional" character and to be an inviting and inspiring place for students and teachers. Designers responded by creating a building that reflects New England's rich architectural tradition, hearkening back to the Federalist period and moving forward through the indigenous Classicism that characterized the region's residential, agricultural, manufacturing, and educational buildings in the 19th and early 20th centuries.

The facility is conceived as a collection of buildings that together create the image of a village, or hill town. (The school's hilltop location underscores this perception.) The assemblage breaks down the scale of this fairly large facility (108,000 square feet, serving a population of 610 students in grades pre-K through 5) into manageable, easily recognizable parts. The parts, in differing though visually coherent ways, echo traditional, regional forms such as sloped roofs and gables and employ a palette of residentially scaled materials—masonry bases, cast stone trim, brick walls, bay windows, gutters, awnings, and white-painted horizontal aluminum siding and trim. The collective yet cohesive form becomes a metaphor for community while playing variations on the dominant architectural traditions of the region.

The highly constrained site dictated a building footprint in which the two classroom wings intersect at an obtuse angle at the main lobby space. Common spaces—media center, cafetorium, gymnasium—are all adjacent to this central space, which serves as an assembly/circulation space for the school and for community functions, like a square or commons at the center of the "school/village." It's here that children assemble and wait for the classroom wings to open at the beginning of each school day, and it's here that parents visiting the school meet and greet one another.

Architecture in the Service of the Spirit. The architecture speaks to the spirit. The lobby's main feature is a column, or tree, from which the geometric organization of the entire school radiates: it is the axis of the plan and therefore the center of the village—the focal point toward which all the massing of the building's constituent parts builds. This tree-form column stands directly below a large circular skylight. Natural light floods down, spotlighting this center area and illuminating the communal area's two-story volume. The central stair rises behind this column, the first landing embracing it with a pulpit-like platform. This platform can be used by a speaker to address students assembling below, but it is also a wonderful place to pause to view the open, sunlit space that is the heart of the school.

Chapter 4

The Elementary School of Today: An Exemplary Educational Specification

[Editor's note: The following educational specification, "The Milton School Educational Design Plan," was developed for an addition/renovation project for Milton Elementary School in Rye, New York. Compiled by Dr. JoAnne Nardone, principal of the Milton School, it represents the input and work of many participants, including faculty representatives Kelly Sheridan and Carol Seltzer; faculty Excellence Team members Dr. Shawn Amdur and Cindy Samperi; and parent Excellence Team members Meg O'Callaghan and Andy Hessekiel (PTO presidents) and Alison Stearns and Cynthia DiPalma. The Rye City Schools' Deputy Superintendent, Dr. Daniel McCann, also contributed to the design plan. Although the program envisioned in this specification was not fully carried out because the project failed at referendum, the original document is an exceptionally thorough, visionary ed spec for an elementary school of today.]

District Mission Statement

The Rye City School District will work in partnership with the community of Rye to ensure that its students become life-long learners and self-reliant, socially responsible, respectful citizens through the creation of a personalized educational environment that challenges and inspires all students to reach their potential and beyond.

Milton School Philosophy

Our fundamental goal is to provide a rigorous and enriching experience for all students. Every child has unique talents and interests and an individual style of learning. Our instructional program fosters each child's intellectual, physical, creative, and moral potential. We also value relationships and encourage social responsibility. Working together with families, we provide a warm, nurturing environment so each teacher and staff member can attend to students' individual needs.

Throughout its 103-year history, Milton School has been acclaimed for academic excellence within a strong, caring community. Our overriding goal for this architectural plan is to launch Milton School to new academic heights. This plan provides the vision, inspiration, and technological infrastructure that will prepare future decades of Milton students to be leaders in this new millennium.

Building Entrance and General Ambiance

Milton School is a showcase for our children's talents and a garden for their creative growth. When our children and their families enter Milton School, they should experience the openness and light that a high ceiling with a small rotunda provides. The foyer could be adorned with imaginative murals and with plants that are cared for by the students (perhaps even through the use of hydroponics).

The school environment should remind our children that they are valued and that their work is important. To support this, hallways should be at least ten feet wide and contain multiple areas for display cases and recessed lighting. Opaque skylighting and large windows providing ample views should be installed at appropriate intervals. (Wide hallways will also foster quick egress in the event of an emergency evacuation.) Soft pastels will create an environment of tranquillity and warmth.

Main Office Complex

The main office complex is the control center of the building. Approximately 1,000 square feet are required to house clerical staff, office equipment, sufficient storage and counter space, the principal's office, and a bathroom. The office should be well lit and airy. A security system with cameras in the hallways and two cameras with different viewpoints in the reception area of the main office will be required.

The main office is also the first area encountered by visitors. It should therefore be at, rather than below, ground level. Benches should be located outside the main office. This complex should be carpeted in the school's official blue. And of course, the decor should reflect the pride we feel for Milton School.

Collaboration is one of the foundations of an outstanding school. Since the principal meets with teachers, parents, and students throughout the day, and teachers and parents collaborate with one another, a 300-square-foot conference room should be located in close proximity to the principal's office. The room should include a computer station with a large-screen, mounted monitor, sufficient wiring for audiovisual equipment, and a large whiteboard.

Nurse's Suite and Psychologist's Office

The nurse helps to maintain the health and well-being of our children and requires workspace of at least 1,000 square feet to attend to their needs and to provide privacy. The space must include both an office and a room for a series of cots, each enclosed by curtains. The nurse's bathroom must be large enough to accommodate children in wheelchairs.

The school psychologist plays a vital role in maintaining the emotional security of our students. She needs a computer station, workspace for a small group session, sufficient shelving, a private telephone line, and a whiteboard (400 square feet required).

To maintain the safety and security of our students, the nurse's suite and psychologist's office should be in close proximity to the principal's office. The psychologist's office must be close to the main entrance so that she is available to children as they enter the building.

Auditorium

Milton School maintains strong ties to the community and has a long tradition of sharing cultural experiences. Students participate in several whole-school assemblies throughout the year and in a comprehensive cultural arts program. Therefore, the new auditorium (which is currently the school's gymnasium) will require 6,000 square feet in order to seat the entire student body (500 students and 50 faculty and staff members) simultaneously. The auditorium should be located on the ground floor at the front of the building, near the main entrance. It should have its own entrance and bathrooms, so that it can be used by the community and other elementary schools for after-school events. The auditorium should have modern sound and lighting systems and adequate dressing and storage areas. It should enable our students to perform and study, aided by the design of its space, light, and acoustics.

Music Suite

Milton School must continue to offer its students a program that addresses the New York State Standards and Rye City School District Music Curriculum. All children in the school perform regularly in concerts and musicals. In addition, all students receive general music instruction. Fourth- and fifth-graders can participate in band, orchestra, or chorus. In some cases, children perform in two or even all three groups. Currently, our district provides students with band and orchestra lessons in the fourth and fifth grades. In the future, third-graders may also participate in band and orchestra. Our school is responsible for over 100 band and orchestra instruments. This number will increase as the school population increases. The instruments require adequate storage in well-ventilated and lighted areas.

Our school is receptive to the opportunities made possible by the Yamaha's Music-in-Education keyboard program, which integrates keyboards into many music classrooms around the country.

The Yamaha program requires one stand-alone computer linked to 15 student keyboards. Students play the keyboards mounted on tables, not keyboard stands. Sufficient power and wiring will be required to accommodate the various cables extended from the keyboard units. Because our music program is also fully committed to the integration of technology, each music room also requires at least four computer stations to enable students to compose and arrange music.

In addition, each music classroom requires a variety of specific equipment in order to provide students with rich and stimulating experiences geared to their age and developmental level. For example, students use a variety of rhythm instruments, both pitched and unpitched, in their daily classes. The general music program recognizes the value and importance of movement in the music curriculum, so students should have sufficient room to move around without bumping into equipment in the room.

Our fifth-graders present a high-quality musical each year. Students audition for parts and rehearse their songs and dances. We require a music suite, auditorium and stage area to support this aspect of the curriculum. The music suite requires sufficient storage (student work samples, both written and audio, must be saved for a period of time) and office space. In addition, two cabinets are required for choral music, and one for orchestral music. The music office requires computer stations for each of the three teachers, with 30-inch monitors and digital video capabilities. The classrooms each need whiteboards and separate built-in storage areas for large and small instruments, and shelving for textbooks, CDs, cassettes and videos. Since students frequently work in a variety of different-sized groups, the rooms should be equipped with modular furniture that can be easily reconfigured. And of course, appropriate acoustics and soundproofing are vital.

To accommodate instrumental music, band and orchestra lessons for grades 3-5, chorus, and the new keyboard program, three music rooms will be required. Two music rooms will require 1,200 square feet each, and the band room will require 800 square feet. A 300-square-foot office and two storage rooms of 200 square feet each are required for costumes and additional instruments. The music suite should be located in close proximity to the auditorium so that students can move easily from the music classrooms to the backstage area.

Primary-Grade Wing
The sixteen primary-grade classes (K-2) should be located on the ground floor in close proximity to each other, with classrooms of the same grade adjacent to each other. The classrooms should surround a courtyard, within which children will have their own garden and worktables.

Primary-grade instruction takes a developmental approach, in which the children have many opportunities to develop critical skills through their learning centers and hands-on activities. Some of the instructional components addressed in the primary grades are:

- Special/mathematical reasoning
- Scientific methods of inquiry
- Creative writing
- Social interaction skills and understanding of communities
- Artistic and musical abilities
- Kinesthetic development
- Honing of small and gross motor skills

The children require ample room to move about in their centers, construct block structures, and socialize. Kindergarten and first grade classrooms require 1,000 square feet with a bathroom within each classroom. Second grade classrooms should be 800 square feet and also contain bathrooms.

All primary-grade classrooms should have walk-in storage closets, wall space for bulletin boards, and storage shelves to accommodate book-binder materials, experience charts and project-related oak tag. They should have sinks and water fountains of appropriate height. Classrooms should have large bulletin boards to display the children's work. Windows should open easily for teachers, yet be child-safe. There should be cubbies with rolling doors in which to store lunchboxes, backpacks, hats, boots, gloves, and coats, and these should be large enough so that the coats do not touch one another. Two-thirds of each classroom should be carpeted; one-third should be covered in linoleum. The carpeting should be removable for cleaning.

Each classroom should contain a separate teacher's desk with a computer workstation and 30-inch mounted television monitor. All classrooms should have cable access and distance video capabilities.

Intermediate-Grade Classes

Classrooms must be 800 square feet and appropriately shaped to enable teachers to work with students in a flexible variety of ways, including with an entire class of students, in guided reading groups, in paired work, while reading alone, and in learning center activities. All classes should contain whiteboards; 30-inch, wall-mounted computer/TV monitors that display analog and digital formats; a DVD or VCR; and separate computer workstation/desks for the teacher. Each classroom should contain large cubbies for students' clothing and backpacks and adequate, secure storage space for instruction materials, equipment, supplies, and student files. All classrooms must have an appropriately scaled sink and water fountain. Classrooms should also be designed so that two classes can be grouped together through the use of high-quality movable doors.

Separate girls' and boys' bathrooms should be located directly outside the classrooms on each floor. The special education classroom should be located in close proximity to the other third-grade classes and contain its own bathroom.

Gym/Cafetasium

The gym will remain at 3,000 square feet and include all required apparatus. A 400-square-foot storage room should be located between the gym and cafetasium, so that the two physical education teachers can share equipment. The cafetasium will serve as both the cafeteria and an additional gymnasium. As a cafeteria, it should seat 200 children comfortably and reflect a feeling of comfort and airiness (3,000 square feet required). The room should contain furniture that can easily be assembled and disassembled. The gym and cafetasium should be located at the rear of the building and provide direct access to the playground. Boys' and girls' bathrooms should be located in the halls directly outside the gym/cafetasium complex.

Faculty Room

The faculty room should be located adjacent to the cafetasium. It should have two computer stations with full technological capabilities, a 30-inch television monitor, and cable access (1,000 square feet required).

Kitchen
1,200 square feet are required.

Technology/Computer Lab
Our teachers are becoming increasingly proficient with computers and are addressing our curricular standards to a greater extent through their use each year. The school must enable its students and teachers to communicate with each other online, and to access the Internet and various school databases. Wiring must be flexible, modular, and capable of supporting wide bandwidths. It should be expandable and scalable and be as easily upgradable to new technological standards as possible. Each classroom should include a separate computer workstation and desk for the teacher's use. The teacher's workstation should include a higher level of security than students' workstations. Each classroom should contain a 30-inch mounted television monitor with full video capabilities and cable access.

The computer lab should be located adjacent to the library/media center and contain 30 workstations arranged in a circular pattern. Tables should be four inches wider than current tables to allow students to place their work next to them. Both a Proxima projector and large-screen monitor should be mounted to the ceiling. The computer lab should have cable access and multimedia capabilities (1,500 square feet required). To provide natural light, exterior windows with vertical blinds are recommended.

A fiber-optic network, capable of conversion to wireless technology in the future, should be installed throughout the building. Sufficient space and temperature control for the fileservers are required.

Library/Media Center
The library/media center should be enlarged to 1,500 square feet. It will function as the hub of the building and be easily accessible from all classrooms. The library/media center should contain eight student computer workstations, two faculty workstations, and two Dynix stations. It should have work areas for both large- and small-group instruction as well as for individual study. Bookshelves will require adequate lighting. The room should include videoconferencing technology, a large-screen monitor mounted to the ceiling, and cable access. A 200-square-foot storage room for audiovisual equipment will also be necessary.

Learning Centers/Support Services
To accommodate a student body of 500, three learning centers (reading/math), one English Language Learners (ELL) center [ELL is a New York State ESL-type program], and one speech and language/occupational therapy/physical therapy center are required. One learning center (reading/math) should be located on each floor in close proximity to the classrooms. Centers require 400 square feet each and must include ample storage. Each center should include one teacher workstation and two student workstations. A 400-square-foot conference room for building-wide Child Study Team conferences is required.

Multipurpose Room

We firmly believe that all students require enrichment experiences differentiated to address their unique talents. The multipurpose room will provide a flexible space for enrichment experiences directly linked to New York State standards. For example, classes may utilize the room as a science lab; improvisational theater; music or science fair; art gallery; living museum; or mock courtroom, session of Congress, national convention, or stock market. This room should have full technology capabilities (1,000 square feet required). The room must also have 200 square feet for storage of a variety of equipment.

Art Studio

The school requires 1,500 square feet, including a movable partition, kiln, and storage space.

Custodial Suite/Custodial Closets

Our head custodian addresses basic carpentry and maintenance. He requires a work area with workbench and storage (800 square feet). The following closets are recommended:

- One grounds storage room (800 square feet)
- One telecommunications closet (150 square feet)
- Three electrical closets (15 square feet)
- Two janitor's sink closets (75 square feet)

Playgrounds

A separate area behind the kindergarten classrooms will be used exclusively by kindergarten students. Benches at the periphery of this area will encourage parents and grandparents to visit. The other two playgrounds should be separated so that one can serve the first and second grades while the other serves grades 3-5.

Storage

Adequate storage space is critical to the efficient implementation of curricular initiatives. In addition to the large storage areas adjacent to the gym/ cafetasium, auditorium, library/media center, and music suite, adequate storage areas on each level are required to store instructional materials, supplies, equipment, and furniture. A small, secure storage area is required off the main office to store standardized testing materials.

Promoting a Comfortable and Healthy Environment

The following are required:

- An HVAC system that provides adequate heating, ventilating, and central air-conditioning (zoned heating and air-conditioning and large, operable windows with screens and access to natural light and outside air).
- Adequate storage space for each floor.

- An effective communication system. (Each classroom should have a telephone and speaker that provide public address capability, emergency outside-line access, and internal private communications linking each teaching space and workspace.)
- Security cameras on each floor.
- Full compliance with the Americans with Disabilities Act (ADA), Occupational Safety and Health Administration (OSHA) regulations, and local fire department requirements. (Although not required in New York State, we are also recommending a building-wide sprinkler system and radon detection system.)
- Traffic flow and parking for 80 vehicles.
- Exterior courtyards, patios, and walks projecting an atmosphere of cleanliness and beauty. (Plantings and shrubbery should be environmentally sound and permit ease of upkeep.)
- Special attention to materials used in plumbing to ensure purity of drinking water. (Water fountains for students should be located directly outside the gym/cafetasium, auditorium, music suite, and library media center.)
- Adequate number and size of student bathrooms on each floor; men's and women's faculty bathrooms on each floor.
- An elevator in close proximity to the main entrance.

Unused Space in the Basement
We would like to use this space for a future pre-K program. Until that time, it will be used for club meetings during and after school, special events, and Parent-Teacher Organization (PTO) activities.

Part II: Creating Schools Collaboratively

Chapter 5

The Process of Creation: In Need of Improvement

Collaboration is essential in the planning and design of new elementary school buildings that will successfully meet future challenges. Too often, though, collaboration gets short-circuited. The creation of a new building—or additions to and renovation of an existing facility—involves a large expenditure of funds and relies on tradition-bound procedures that can get in the way of "outside-the-box" innovation. Checks and balances incorporated into the process are aimed primarily at containing costs and often provide little room for educational or architectural vision.

In this chapter, we closely examine the typical process of creating a new elementary school, commenting on its inherent flaws and suggesting ways in which it could be improved. Although the process outlined here varies somewhat depending on its location, it is essentially the way a new public school is created anywhere in the country. The major steps in any such process are these:

1. Getting the idea off the ground
2. Developing an educational specification (perhaps with a consultant's assistance)
3. Earning approval from the state department of education (and the state legislature, when required)
4. Hiring an architect
5. Gaining passage of a referendum, followed by the design and construction process itself

In reviewing this process—with an eye toward discovering how it could work better—two things must be kept especially in mind:

*   *The educational specification plays a crucially important role in a project's success.* A good "ed spec" pays heed to the interests of all the "stakeholders" in the project. It incorporates the community's vision of the future. It gives the architect sufficient guidance to design a facility that will truly meet present and future educational needs. And, if it is well written and used effectively, the educational specification can be a primary tool in convincing local voters to pass a school-building referendum. (For more on educational specifications for elementary schools, see Chapter 9.)
*   *Democratic collaboration—and a process that fosters it—requires leadership at all levels:* from parents, faculty, school principals and other administrators, superintendents, local government leaders, state boards of education, and state legislators. Changing the time-honored mechanisms by which new schools come into being requires an adventurous spirit and some risk-taking, and all participants must envision, and experiment with, ways of making both the process and the product better. Beyond this, an improved process will require at least one "point person" to ensure continuity throughout the life of the project, from the inception of the idea through the completion of construction. Although we believe that this role falls most naturally to the district

superintendent, we have occasionally seen it fulfilled by a well-informed committee chairperson who has the time and dedication commensurate with the task.

Inception

Let's begin our look at the process from the moment that a new facility is first thought of. It's easy to imagine the initial conversation, which usually occurs in an administrator's office—most likely the district superintendent's, but sometimes that of a school principal. The issue driving the conversation is sometimes a problematic, antiquated existing facility, but it's more likely that expanding enrollment or a programmatic space need is what precipitates the interchange.

The conversation between superintendent and principal might go something like this: The principal speaks of how desperately a new facility is needed, and the superintendent responds,

"Joe, I know we need it, but this is an election year!" or

"Joe, we sure need it but I'm about ready to put a budget on the table and I don't want to raise more eyebrows," or

"Joe, I know we need it, but last year the town council asked us to hold off on capital projects."

At about the same time that this kick-off conversation is happening, the Parent/Teacher Association is also starting to focus on the problem, claiming, "We've got to put our kids first. We can afford a new building, and we shouldn't wait any longer."

Then, an aspiring politician—maybe a town council-type with young children—will start beating the drum. The dawning possibility of creating a new school is debated in backroom conversations, as community leaders join the discussion and start to probe—perhaps even visiting the existing school to assess the realities of the situation for themselves.

[Comment: The local political forces frequently pay little attention to enrollment projections and need statements prepared by educators. Often, municipal leaders wait until classrooms—or pipes!—are bursting before even considering a major facility expenditure. They do not, in general, trust educators, feeling that the best way to keep expenditures—both operating and capital—down is to squeeze the system until undeniable evidence of underfunding presents itself. This reactive philosophy is pervasive throughout the facility creation process. Building committees may repeatedly pressure the educators, architects, and contractors to "sharpen their pencils" to reduce costs, and this becomes far more important than meeting students' needs in a timely fashion or taking steps to ensure a quality design.]

The Educational Specification

The description of the project is usually called the educational specification—"ed spec," for short. Some ed specs are highly developed and detailed documents (running from 20 to 30 pages) that give clear direction; others are a page long and require an interpretation process that entails significant discussion and a great deal of imagination.

[Comment: School districts frequently need guidance on how to write a good, useful educational specification. It is helpful for state departments of education to give a detailed description of what is required in a specification. Early cost and square-footage estimates, if they are accurate, can cause trouble when the project starts.]

State Approval Process

In our state, Connecticut, the State Department of Education requires a project application one year in advance of state legislative approval of a facility. The infamous ED049 facility application form—generally thought of as a "placeholder"—must be approved by both the local board of education and the municipal legislative body prior to submission. The 049 form asks the superintendent of schools to identify the problem and to obtain an estimate of the cost of correcting it. Further, the form asks the local district to estimate state reimbursement in accordance with a funding formula based on the town's or city's socioeconomic need and adjusted for the size of the student body and whether the project involves an elementary, middle, or high school.

A town or board of education will usually bring an architect on board to help in preparing the 049 form. At this stage, architects often offer predesign services, hoping to develop a relationship with the district with the aim of getting a contract for the project once the approval process has been completed. The architect treads a fine line in developing project costs—keeping one eye on the salability of the bottom-line figure and the other on how well the educational specification will be met. Having to return to the State Department of Education for additional funds after initial approval is not desirable.

In almost all cases, state reimbursement does not cover all components of a project: for example, the state might refuse to reimburse part of a project on the grounds that that portion of the building (e.g., a portion of the auditorium) is not "educational" or that planned space is more lavish than what is necessary to meet basic needs. Just how far above state reimbursement levels a project can go is always an interesting question. Decisions to include nonreimbursable components are usually based on an analysis of state reimbursements and on the town's desire and ability to support education beyond that level. It's not uncommon for a wealthier town to decide to build a more expensive and lavish facility because its citizens want "the best" for their children (and, of course, because the town can afford to do so).

The State Education Commissioner may waive reimbursement requirements for good and sufficient reason—and, in fact, the Commissioner regularly does waive them for magnet schools, as well as for urban schools that need a wide variety of special spaces relating, for example, to bilingual education, the orientation of students who are recent immigrants, special education, and/or behavior/security problems.

Submission of the 049 form is routinely put off until the last minute—June 30 (that is, the end of the fiscal year)—because town bodies rarely act unless faced with a deadline.

[Comment: Availability of state-reimbursed preliminary feasibility study funding would allow for a more thorough startup process and would produce 049 documents that more accurately represent what the facilities that are ultimately built will actually be like.]

The state legislature's approval of the project is usually routine and based on the State Department of Education's recommendations. Legislators often talk of capping the amount of money to be authorized. They also talk of revising state standards and funding formulas. Historically, however, no action has been taken—other than to put local legislators and superintendents on notice that delaying submission of a project might mean having to face revised legislation in a subsequent year.

[Comment: Legislators spend most of their time worrying about levels of expenditure—and very little time reviewing and second-guessing the state approval process or looking at the actual projects. Under its own time pressure, the State Department of Education has little time during the approvals process to examine educational specifications, choosing instead to focus on enrollment validation and on questions of what will and will not be reimbursed. The state department could help the process by providing a database of existing project statistics that would be useful to architects, educators, boards of education, and building committees. For instance, comparative square-footage data is not presently available on either a state or a national basis. Such a database could outline exemplary educational specifications. One district, for instance, could look at the science lab or media center solution achieved by another district (in the state or somewhere else in the country).]

The Building Committee
After the 049 form is approved, the town leadership usually passes the project on to a building committee (sometimes, a town council will itself serve as the building committee). Some towns have permanent building committees. Others appoint committees to work on specific projects. Occasionally, a committee includes representation from the local board of education, but more routinely the committee is made up of local contractors, lawyers, architects, engineers, teachers, and educational advocates. In

many cases the local taxpayer association is represented. (In an ideal situation, all these constituencies would be represented.)

The building committee usually relies on board of education approval of the specification or concept when accepting the project and routinely interprets its charge as building "to the spec"—not identifying and/or interpreting educational needs.

The Architect

Before engaging an architect, the building committee, with assistance from an administrative clerk of the town, issues a request for proposal (RFP) in accordance with state and local laws regarding bidding and hiring. Hiring a professional architect does not require choosing the lowest fee, but the price of service is frequently a central consideration in making a selection.

[Comment: As an alternative to a bottom-line based selection process, the qualifications-based selection (QBS) process should be considered.]

The architect responds to the RFP with a booklet submission describing the firm, including bios of the team that will work on the project, and outlining why the firm is suited for the job. Based on its review of the submissions it receives, the building committee often selects four or five architectural firms to "short list" and schedules interviews with these firms. The architectural firm may designate a team—typically consisting of a principal of the firm, a project manager, a project architect, a designer, an engineer, a landscape architect, and perhaps other participants—to attend the interview, which usually lasts from half an hour to an hour. Alternatively, the firm may be represented more simply by a principal and a selected team member.

During the consideration process, the building committee may check firms' references, visit facilities (completed or under construction) designed by the short-listed firms, and sometimes visit the architects' offices.

[Comment: Unfortunately, most superintendents of schools elect not to be involved in this part of the process—and, in fact, don't even bother to designate someone from the superintendent's office to participate in building committee meetings. This is a real mistake, since the superintendent—or his or her designee—can be the "glue" that holds together the goals of the board of education, the town, and the building committee.]

The Referendum

Most towns are required by local charter to have a public vote, or referendum, approving the particular project. Needless to say, voters will want as much information as possible before offering up their "yea" or "nay."

Unfortunately, in most cases voters have trouble getting the information they need in order to decide whether the expenditure is wise and whether the projected facility will really meet students' needs. Voters who go to the building committee seeking information will most likely encounter what amounts to "buck-passing." Most building committees don't want to spend money developing information on an unapproved project, so they turn the matter over to the architect. But most architects are unwilling to do extensive design work on an unapproved project, which may be voted down, and so the architect refers to the specification, which was created by the superintendent of schools and approved by the board of education and the town legislative body to facilitate the filling-out of the infamous 049 form—and which is therefore likely to be an inadequate description of the project!

[Comment: In the referendum environment, facility-development rationales are usually based on enrollment needs, the age of an existing facility, and affordability concerns—not on educational or programmatic issues. (Unsurprisingly, referendum issues tend to revolve around how much the property tax rate will increase if the facility is approved.) It doesn't have to be this way. The educational specification, if it were written well and clearly stated programmatic needs, could serve as the centerpiece of a referendum-approval rationale.

We cannot overemphasize the importance of the superintendent's leadership during the referendum phase. Unfortunately, exercising such leadership requires a great deal of time—which may be in very short supply—and it can be politically dangerous. Frequently, the superintendent, not having the time to spend, and concerned about political ramifications, will simply stand aside. In this leadership vacuum, the blunt logic of dollars and cents may take over—and the need to improve educational programs may get lost.

Of course, a good architect will attempt to provide the needed leadership, but, absent strong support from the superintendent, the architect will lack the local knowledge and the clout to speak on behalf of the program. Well-intentioned architects do their best to meet specification needs and provide a quality product, but they're mostly forced to bend to the wind when cost issues prevail.]

Conclusion

As we've seen, the process by which new educational facilities are currently created in Connecticut (and in much of the rest of the country, as well) is seriously flawed. Responsibility is passed from authority to authority. Educational specifications are often poorly developed. As a result, students' needs and educational vision are given short shrift. But, as we hope we've also conveyed, the process can be greatly improved.

For starters, the State Department of Education could be of enormous help if it were to provide comparative (state and national) square-footage data, if it were to require submission of a detailed educational specification in the initial approval process, and if it were to review that specification thoroughly before making a recommendation to the legislature. (Legislators, too, would do well to concern themselves at least as much with educational vision as they do with expenditures.)

Ideally, the development of an ed spec should be a highly collaborative process involving all the stakeholders in the community. Often, architects are asked to do more than design and oversee construction of a facility; they are asked to participate in the development of educational specifications. This isn't necessarily a bad thing, but having the architect develop and market educational specifications without appropriate support from the educational staff and other stakeholders can be counterproductive.

As it stands today, the process of facility creation tends to limit educational vision, architectural creativity, and the community's ability to meet student needs. Given the prevailing bottom-line orientation, it is ironic that flaws inherent in the existing process may actually wind up costing the taxpayer more rather than less, as poorly envisioned schools demonstrate their inadequacy over time.

Chapter 6

Collaboration in the Development of Educational Specifications

A first-rate, useful educational specification ("ed spec") does four things:

1. *It describes the vision motivating the creation of the new facility (or renovation or addition) and its place in the wider community, incorporating the perspectives of all of the facility's stakeholders.*
2. *It provides an objective, quantifiable rationale for the new facility, drawing on and citing demographic information about anticipated enrollments and the character of the student body over the coming years.*
3. *It presents a detailed, thorough list of programmatic requirements and of the spaces that will be needed to implement the program, paying close attention to the school's programmatic needs and operational capabilities.*
4. *It provides a base of information for developing an estimate of "net" (program) space and "gross" (support space) and a related total project cost.*
5. *It generates excitement and enthusiasm for the new facility throughout the community.*

Although the ed spec ultimately functions as *the* primary resource used by the architect in designing the building, it is vitally important to remember that the educational specification is an *educational*, not an architectural, document. Some districts produce ed specs that are too vague—specs that fail to identify program needs and related projected enrollments. But some school districts go too far, wasting time by suggesting design approaches that may not be used or construction items that may not be needed in the creation of the actual facility.

There is no single method for producing a good, useful ed spec: different districts take different approaches, any of which might be successful. Some districts rely on the superintendent of schools to write the educational specification, and, if the superintendent devotes energy to the task, is a good writer, and is diligent in seeking others' input, this method may produce a superior ed spec. Many districts, however, hire consultants to guide them through this sometimes challenging process. Some architectural firms offer such consulting services, and, in an important sense, an architect is a natural choice, since many architectural firms can draw on a wealth of historical data and technical resources and because it is an architect who will ultimately have to use the specification to develop drawings. But, no matter who is providing the consulting service, that firm will have to turn to the educational staff and other stakeholders for information relevant to that particular school project.

In fact, although any of these approaches might work well, the one rule that *any* ed spec development process should follow is *to invite the early and ongoing involvement of all of the new facility's stakeholders*. And there is no getting around the fact that soliciting their participation—and thereby generating their enthusiasm—is a lengthy and complex process that, to succeed, must be carefully managed. As we stress again and again in this book, democracy takes time and requires skilled leadership.

Step 1: The Vision

Don't make the mistake of dismissing the *vision* that guides the creation of a new facility as "the soft stuff." The facts and figures come later, but articulating a comprehensive vision of educational philosophy and of the facility's role in the life of the wider community is *the absolutely essential first step in producing a successful ed spec.* Drafting a vision statement helps the community to see where it is headed, to organize its priorities, to investigate new approaches to education and curriculum design (and to decide which of these will best serve its children), and—at its very best—to boldly address the challenges that the community believes the future will bring. In a sense, everything else—from the size of the gymnasium to the openness of the school to the wider community of users—follows from the vision guiding the building's planning, design, and construction.

The best vision statements are extremely thorough, addressing virtually every aspect of the curriculum and the building's non-education-related functions *but stopping short* of specifying the numbers and kinds of spaces necessary to implement the vision. The vision statement gives the community the opportunity to be ambitious, hopeful, forward-looking—in a word, *visionary*. This is not to say that the vision should be unrealistic—and, in fact, a certain amount of realism regarding budgetary and operational issues will naturally be imposed by the collaborative process by which the vision statement comes into being.

Although the language of the statement itself is likely to be drafted by a small group of people or even by a single individual (perhaps the superintendent), it should represent the work and collective thinking of the entire community. Gathering that knowledge is best accomplished through a series of conversations and meetings with the various constituencies—students, principal and administrative staff, faculty, other school staff, taxpayers and community groups, and so on. There's no hard-and-fast requirement regarding the format of such conversations and meetings: some might be set up as "town hall"-type hearings that the entire community is invited to attend, others might be intensive focus groups with limited numbers of staff or parents, others might be one-on-one conversations between the superintendent and the school principal and faculty members. Consultants generally come equipped with strategies for gathering this input effectively, but it's clear that such methods should be tailored to the needs of the specific community and school and the working styles of superintendent, principal, and faculty. What's also clear is that—for the entire community's wishes, needs, desires, and insights to be genuinely represented in the final vision statement—many separate meetings may be entailed.

There's no easy way to categorize (or limit) the kinds of questions that might be considered during such exchanges, except to say that they should be somewhat broad and general in scope. Here are just a few examples:

1. What are our projected enrollments for five, ten, and fifteen years from now? Are the community's demographics changing, and how? Should we anticipate a greater (or lesser) need for ESL programs, for example, or cultural orientation programs for recent-immigrant students? Is the demand for special education-related components likely to grow more intense in the coming years?

2. How much technology is desired at the elementary level—and is this consistent with technology plans for the district's middle and high schools?

3. To what extent should the community's cultural diversity, or lack of it, influence the curriculum?

4. How should the school be organized? For example, if the new facility is a large school, will it be organized as a single school or divided into a number of teams or houses?

5. How will the wider community use the building? Will it be a place where town meetings will be held? Will the media center be open to the general public during certain hours? Will community arts groups be using the auditorium or other spaces? (And so on.)

Step 2: The Program
Once the vision statement has been prepared, it's time to begin translating the broad agenda that it lays out into the specifics of spaces, the numbers of students (and other facility users) who will occupy them, and the key relationships among spaces that will best achieve the vision statement's curricular and other programmatic goals. (By "key relationships," we mean things like adjacencies: for example, should the media center be contiguous to the main lobby in order to facilitate use by the wider community?)

Of course, the superintendent or ed spec consultant (perhaps working hand in hand with a "vision committee") will already have begun to gather some of this kind of information: it's inevitable that the vision of the new school facility will have been shaped by an awareness of the character and size of the student body, for example. But, until now, the process should have steered clear of developing specific programmatic solutions.

The key to devising these programmatic solutions successfully is—once again— *a collaborative process*. The principle motivating a collaborative approach is a simple one: the stakeholders in any given curricular or extra-curricular area are not just the people who have the greatest investment in that area, they're also the people who have the greatest knowledge about what it will take to implement the vision statement's agenda in that area. Thus, particular faculty and administrators knowledgeable in specific areas contribute ideas to help answer questions like the following:

- What is our special education strategy?
- Should we have a separate, dedicated cafeteria and auditorium, or a combination "cafetorium"?
- How much emphasis will we place on the arts? Should we have dedicated

art and music classrooms? Do we need separate choral and instrumental rooms?

- What about science? Will science instruction occur in regular classrooms, or do we need a purpose-built science lab?

During this phase of the ed spec's development, the vision statement should guide the approach to the "operational realities." But efficient use of the *entire* physical plant should be a goal, since no community will want to pay for an overdesigned facility (a "Taj Mahal") or one in which all program areas are accorded too much space.

Once a complete list of required/desired spaces and a description of the population(s) that will use those spaces have been compiled, it's better to stop and wait for the architect to assign rough square footages to the spaces. If the person or committee developing the ed spec (without an architect's assistance) goes ahead and assigns square-footage numbers to the list of spaces, it's quite likely that the architect hired to design the building will have to revisit the matter, meeting with all the people involved in order to test the assumptions they used to determine size. (In plain terms, it's probably a waste of time for anyone but an architect to assign square-footage numbers to the project's components.)

Despite the fact that any new elementary school building will be "customized" to meet a given community's specific educational needs and vision, those charged with the development of an educational specification may find it very helpful to have some sort of model to work from, or to play their own ideas off against. Later in this book, we provide just such a model—a somewhat generic, though comprehensive, elementary ed spec. (See Chapter 9.)

From the Abstract to the Concrete

Once the programmatic details of the ed spec have been developed, it's time to begin assigning "numbers" to the project—first, square footages; then, dollar estimates of the cost of the facility as outlined in the spec. If the district has retained an architect to help develop the ed spec, this stage represents a continuation of the process; if not, this is the moment when an architect must be brought on board to begin translating the desires embodied in the ed spec into the actualities of size and budget.

It may be somewhat surprising to those unfamiliar with the process, but, once the architect has been given a list of desired spaces and probable occupancies, it's a fairly routine matter to determine the probable square footages of each of those spaces and, in turn, the probable gross and net square footages of the entire facility. (The "net" consists of all the space that will be used for programmatic purposes; the "gross" includes all the other space—corridor space, infrastructure space, and so on and on—that will be needed to make the facility function.) An experienced architect will draw on a wealth of historical data to make these determinations.

From there, it is again a fairly routine matter to come up with a ballpark cost for the building. Here, it's a matter of applying historical data *plus* comprehensive knowledge of the construction market in a given area or region, and any good estimator—whether the estimator is part of the architect's team, or a construction manager, or an independent estimating firm—will be able, once the square footages have been calculated, to apply the necessary formulas and to work out a fairly accurate construction budget, both for the entire facility and for each of its major components. These numbers won't be perfectly precise, of course, and a budget at this stage of development typically includes a "design contingency" line item to cover unknowns. (Estimates will become much more accurate after design has been performed, when estimators will be able to calculate amounts of building materials needed, labor time for specific trades, and so on.) But these "rough" numbers will be good enough to guide further decision-making.

What *further* decision-making? Well, experience shows that the specific programmatic desires articulated in an ed spec often outdistance the amount of money that a community can actually afford—or the amount that the voters are likely to approve in a referendum. It isn't until this point in the process—when the "rough" (though surprisingly accurate) construction cost estimates are in—that decision-makers can begin to adjust the ed spec's program to the financial realities that the community faces.

Often, the community's governing body or town leaders will have begun this whole process with a certain maximum budget in mind. If that figure is, say, $15 million and the rough estimate comes in at $20 million, then it's necessary to return to the ed spec and begin prioritizing, distinguishing between "needs" and "wants," culling less-essential program elements, and looking for ways in which spaces can be put to multiple use—anything, in other words, that will reduce the amount of space and therefore the construction cost while maintaining as much of the desired program as possible.

This, too, is a collaborative process, and there's often some room for negotiation between the building committee or board of education and the community's political leadership. It may, in other words, be possible to salvage at least some of the elements that cause the envisioned facility to exceed the original budget limit. And it bears pointing out that this kind of negotiation is made all the easier *if* the process has been collaborative from the very beginning, since all the stakeholders—including those who hold the purse strings—will have been involved in envisioning the new school building and will want it to match as closely as possible all the accumulating expectations and hopes.

In fact, that's a *key* insight—and a good way to end this chapter before turning to collaboration during the design and project management stages. As we said earlier, one of the chief reasons to do the ed spec right is *to generate excitement and enthusiasm for the new facility throughout the community.* If all the stakeholders feel that they've participated in the ed spec's development—and if they all have some understanding of the new facility's potential benefits to the entire community—they'll be much more willing to go the extra mile to make the building as good as possible. When they've been an integral part of the process, town council members are more likely to understand the need for a particular program element and to increase the allowable budget accordingly. And voters will be much more likely to respond positively when the matter is put before them in a referendum. A good ed spec is good politics. *It builds community.*

Chapter 7

Collaborative Design and Project Management

Tomorrow's educational environments must accommodate new approaches to teaching and learning while serving the needs of all of a facility's "stakeholders"—that is, the members of the community who have an interest in the outcome of the project.

The U.S. Department of Education has identified six design principles for the planning and designing of schools that also serve as centers of the community. These principles have been endorsed by the American Institute of Architects (AIA), the Council for Educational Facilities Planners International (CEFPI), Urban Educational Facilities for the 21st Century (UEF), and the American Association of Retired Persons (AARP). The principles challenge architects to design learning environments that:

1. Enhance teaching and learning and accommodate the needs of all learners
2. Serve as a center of the community
3. Result from a planning/design process involving all stakeholders
4. Provide for health, safety, and security
5. Make effective use of all available resources
6. Allow for flexibility and adaptability to changing needs

The architects and educators of Fletcher-Thompson, Inc., have developed architectural planning and design solutions that give concrete expression to these abstract concepts. We believe that our approach to school building planning and design can serve as a model for other educators, planners, and architects—and for communities across the country—as we enter the new millennium.

Design Approach

Time and again, our extensive experience in the planning and design of school facilities has proved that the process by which a project is initiated is critical to its overall success. We have come to believe that a major factor contributing to a project's success is to organize the project properly from the very start. A well-organized project—led by an expertly staffed team—ensures that a district's educational goals of quality, cost, and schedule can be fulfilled.

The importance of continued community support over the life of a project cannot be overemphasized. Neither should we underestimate the pressures placed on municipal governments and local school districts with regard to costs and the performance of their facilities. Today, better-informed, better-educated voters are holding building committees and municipal and school officials accountable for both first-time costs and long-term performance of construction projects.

To maximize project value and to minimize maintenance and operating costs, important decisions regarding cost and overall quality must be made early in the design process and must be clearly communicated to all participants.

The goal, here, is to minimize the need for changes late in the design process, when such changes are decidedly less effective and may compromise the project's quality or scope.

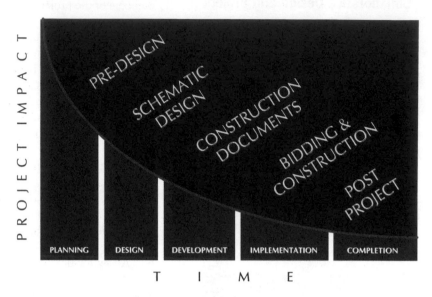

The creation of a new elementary school is a complex process involving the balancing of many variables. The following list of design-related issues, arranged by category, is not necessarily complete, but it does show the wide scope of issues that should be brought to the table from the very start of the design process. (Note that these are general issues, not specific educational/programmatic issues.)

Mission
- Define expectations
- Understand the difference between traditional and contemporary architecture
- Create a sense of cohesiveness
- Represent vision for the future
- Understand the role of the building in its community

Community Use
- Welcome community to the campus
- Create well-defined entrances and internal pathways
- Integrate the needs of multiple users: students, parents, faculty, administrators, community groups, continuing education programs, etc.
- Provide appropriate levels of security, indoors and out, for both daytime and nighttime use

Building Context and Massing
- Understand the site-its limitations and potential
- Understand site preparation/remediation issues

- Understand environmental issues
- Harmonize larger and smaller built elements, creating a variety of scales
- Integrate building and landscape

Building Materials
- Use local materials, whenever possible
- Provide a sense of place through the use of materials
- Develop a unifying and distinctive design vocabulary
- Emphasize interplay of texture, shade, shadow, color, and light
- Understand the interaction of natural and artificial lighting
- Understand the importance of accents

Landscaping
- Configure building elements in a way that defines outdoor spaces
- Specify maintainable planting program
- Develop designs consistent with all standards for outdoor lighting and furnishings
- Provide flexibility for special events
- Understand the impact of landscaping decisions on security issues

Entrance and Circulation
- Provide a strong, identifiable "front door"
- Provide multiple, adequately lighted entrances that can be access-controlled as necessary
- Provide for safe and accessible drop-offs by bus and car
- Provide for clarity of circulation, with an appropriate hierarchy of main lobbies and halls, primary and secondary corridors
- Assist orientation within the building by providing views to the exterior

Memorable Places
- Create multiple scales and well-proportioned spaces, some comfortable for individuals, some for small groups, and some for large groups
- Allow for linked activities and flexibility of use
- Design the entire facility in a comfortable way—one that uses natural light, color, and architectural richness to enhance the learning process

Technology and Infrastructure
- Provide adequate infrastructure for high-speed, broadband communications
- Anticipate the coming wireless revolution, providing convenient access unencumbered by plug-ins
- Incorporate federally mandated firewalling standards
- Consider high-resolution monitors for large-group Internet viewing
- Consider high-resolution readers for textbook download/display

- Consider acoustical aids for hearing-impaired students in electronic presentation spaces (computer labs, language labs)
- Incorporate space for technology management
- Incorporate space for repair and disbursement of equipment and software downloads

Special Education (and related) Needs
- Take all relevant federal, state, and local laws and mandates into account
- Incorporate access aids for physically disabled students throughout
- Ensure that physical education and sports facilities allow for disabled access
- Incorporate "refuge" spaces (for wheelchair-bound students) in corridors
- Provide Braille signage for visually impaired users
- Incorporate space for electric wheelchair recharging stations
- Provide adequate Planning and Placement Team meeting space
- Provide conference space for anger management and dispute mediation

Health, Safety, and Security
- Ensure superior indoor air quality and climate control
- Provide for safe drop off, storage, and pick up of coats, musical instruments, other personal belongings (laptops, etc.)
- Provide appropriate, adequate lighting throughout
- Provide for ease of adult supervision and direct visual monitoring throughout the facility and site
- Consider and select from range of electronic security technologies; anticipate possible use of facial recognition or other ID technology

The design process is an educative process for all the participants. At its best, it encourages attention to detail in the following areas:

- Understanding of building materials
- Appreciation for cost/value relationship
- Care about maintenance and operations

Fletcher Thompson's design approach is intentionally geared toward fostering this attention to detail. For example, architects and engineers typically evaluate both first-time cost and long-term performance when selecting and recommending building systems and products to the building committee and building users. We present only time-tested and thoroughly researched options to the decision-makers, and we frequently provide samples for more extensive testing to maintenance personnel prior to finalizing any decisions. This process affords building committees the opportunity to make informed decisions. Economy and design are not mutually exclusive; they are balanced through "value." Through the creative combination of commonly available, durable materials and carefully selected colors, an exciting design can be produced at minimal cost.

Collaboration

The beginning of a project provides the rare opportunity to make sure that the problems are correctly identified and that they will be creatively solved. The beginning of a project also provides an opportunity for soliciting input into the design and planning activities from the entire community of users. A new elementary school facility is certain to have quite a diverse set of stakeholders. Stakeholders are likely to include the following (and possibly others):

1. Students
2. Building committee members
3. The Board of Education
4. The superintendent and district administrators
5. Municipal government agencies and officials
6. The principal and school administrators
7. Faculty and staff
8. Parents
9. Taxpayers
10. Local business people
11. Community groups
12. Community leaders

Because of this diversity, we utilize an integrative process that includes workshops designed to promote the stakeholders' active participation. The goal of this collaborative process is to achieve "buy-in" on the part of all participants. Sharing the "authorship" of the project strengthens the sense of community and contributes to a successful building project.

Ensuring that the needs of the entire community of users are met requires the following:

1. An interactive process involving all stakeholders
2. An open exchange of ideas with workshops and focus groups
3. An emphasis on listening to what is being said
4. Establishing a common frame of reference
5. Gaining consensus regarding the educational program
6. Establishing a vocabulary of materials and furnishings
7. Early identification of key milestones
8. Previewing all information prior to design review and progress meetings so timely decisions can be made
9. Ongoing dialogue about design alternatives
10. Balancing design goals with budget criteria throughout project development
11. Continuity of the core team to ensure successful implementation of ideas from design through construction

A series of study tools and deliverables, including the following, keeps decision-makers informed:

- Specific meeting agendas, meeting minutes, and monthly status reports
- 2-D diagrams and computer-generated 3-D images to document key programmatic relationships
- Simplistic models for critical design issues
- Bubble diagrams and conceptual drawings
- Image boards
- Site visits to comparable facilities
- Samples to discuss materials and aesthetic considerations (e.g., color consistency)
- System diagrams to ensure constructability, meet code requirements, and anticipate maintenance issues
- Design plans at all key milestones
- Presentation materials and renderings

Project Management

Throughout the design and construction process, thousands of decisions are made that affect the quality, cost, and completion date of the final product. To successfully manage a project and communicate information to the members of the architectural team in a timely fashion, Fletcher Thompson utilizes customized project management tools, including a Task Schedule and a Master Control Budget. These tools help answer the important questions:

- What is to be done?
- Who will complete the task?
- When must it be done?
- How much will it cost?
- What happens if work isn't completed on time?

Task Schedule. The Task Schedule lists and schedules tasks to be accomplished throughout the project process. This allows team members to remain focused on the big picture while clarifying the steps necessary to get there.

Meeting the aggressive schedule imposed on a school-construction project necessitates a clear and organized decision-making process. The Task Schedule shows when all the necessary decisions must be made in order to meet project goals.

One of the first tasks on the Schedule is the Project Kick-Off Workshop. In this meeting, the roles and responsibilities of all team members are established and the decision-making process is defined and agreed to. This consensus is critical to ensure the seamless flow of information and approvals necessary to move the project forward expeditiously.

The schedule is a dynamic document that also tracks the tasks as work progresses, allowing for proactive management to keep the project on schedule to meet the project's goals.

The sample Task Schedule included here shows the major milestones that would occur in virtually any school construction project. Of course, such schedules are tailored, expanded, and developed for specific projects and their integral components, incorporating the input of all the project team members.

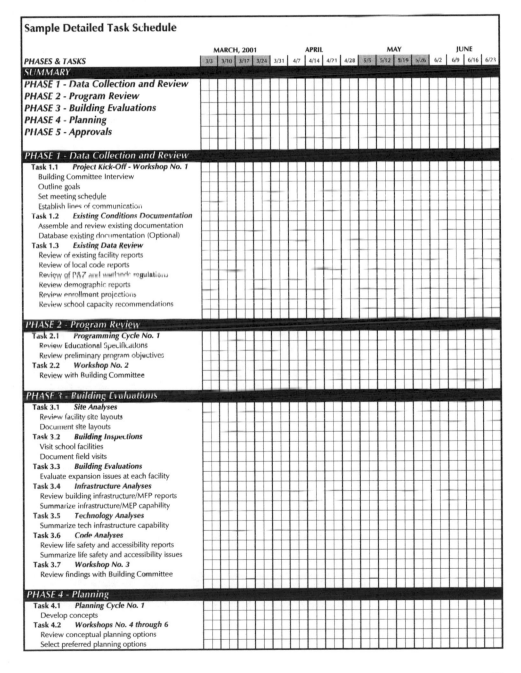

Sample Detailed Task Schedule

PHASES & TASKS	MARCH, 2001					APRIL				MAY					JUNE		
	3/3	3/10	3/17	3/24	3/31	4/7	4/14	4/21	4/28	5/5	5/12	5/19	5/26	6/2	6/9	6/16	6/23
SUMMARY																	
PHASE 1 - Data Collection and Review																	
PHASE 2 - Program Review																	
PHASE 3 - Building Evaluations																	
PHASE 4 - Planning																	
PHASE 5 - Approvals																	
PHASE 1 - Data Collection and Review																	
Task 1.1 Project Kick-Off - Workshop No. 1																	
Building Committee Interview																	
Outline goals																	
Set meeting schedule																	
Establish lines of communication																	
Task 1.2 Existing Conditions Documentation																	
Assemble and review existing documentation																	
Database existing documentation (Optional)																	
Task 1.3 Existing Data Review																	
Review of existing facility reports																	
Review of local code reports																	
Review of P&Z and wetlands regulations																	
Review demographic reports																	
Review enrollment projections																	
Review school capacity recommendations																	
PHASE 2 - Program Review																	
Task 2.1 Programming Cycle No. 1																	
Review Educational Specifications																	
Review preliminary program objectives																	
Task 2.2 Workshop No. 2																	
Review with Building Committee																	
PHASE 3 - Building Evaluations																	
Task 3.1 Site Analyses																	
Review facility site layouts																	
Document site layouts																	
Task 3.2 Building Inspections																	
Visit school facilities																	
Document field visits																	
Task 3.3 Building Evaluations																	
Evaluate expansion issues at each facility																	
Task 3.4 Infrastructure Analyses																	
Review building infrastructure/MEP reports																	
Summarize infrastructure/MEP capability																	
Task 3.5 Technology Analyses																	
Summarize tech infrastructure capability																	
Task 3.6 Code Analyses																	
Review life safety and accessibility reports																	
Summarize life safety and accessibility issues																	
Task 3.7 Workshop No. 3																	
Review findings with Building Committee																	
PHASE 4 - Planning																	
Task 4.1 Planning Cycle No. 1																	
Develop concepts																	
Task 4.2 Workshops No. 4 through 6																	
Review conceptual planning options																	
Select preferred planning options																	

Master Control Budget. Fletcher Thompson maintains a high level of commitment to managing the cost of its projects throughout the design process. To ensure that the budget reflects the most up-to-date and accurate cost data available, we typically draw from the firm's historical construction cost database, reference published cost-estimating resources, and seek the help

MASTER CONTROL BUDGET

	Quantity	Units	Cost/SF	Total	Eligible Cost	32.00%
I. CAPITAL CONSTRUCTION COSTS (HARD COSTS)						
1.1 Site Development		SF		$	$	
New Construction		SF		$	$	%
Field Repair				$	$	%
1.2 Off Site Improvements				$		%
1.3 Building Construction				$	$	
New Construction		SF		$	$	
Lower Level		SF		$		
Level Two		SF		$		
Level Three		SF		$		
Renovations		SF		$	$	
Lower Level				$		
Level Two				$		
Level Three				$	$	%
1.4 Change Order Allowance	%			$	$	%
1.5 Contingency	%			$	$	%
1.6 CM Fees/Reimbursables	%			$	$	%
SUBTOTAL CAPITAL CONSTRUCTION COSTS				$	$	%
II. OTHER CAPITAL COSTS						
2.1 Land Acquisition				$	$	%
2.2 Furniture and Furnishings		student		$	$	%
2.3 Computer Station Hardware		each		$	$	%
2.4 Front End Equipment, Servers				$	$	%
2.5 Telephone, Computer Wiring				$		%
2.6 TV Distribution Wiring				$	$	%
2.7 Security System Wiring				$	$	%
2.8 Miscellaneous Equipment				$	$	%
SUBTOTAL OTHER CAPITAL COSTS			$	$	$	%
III. EXPENSES (SOFT COSTS)						
3.1 Architectural and Engineering Fees				$	$	%
3.2 Specialty Consultants				$	$	%
3.3 Testing/Special Inspections				$	$	%
3.4 Surveys and Borings				$	$	%
3.5 Reimbursable Expenses				$	$	%
3.6 Full Time CA, Clerk of the Works				$	$	%
3.7 Moving and Storage				$	$	%
3.8 Bid Printing and Advertising				$	$	%
3.9 Rendering, Models				$	$	
SUBTOTAL OF EXPENSES			$	$	$	%
IV. BUDGET SUBTOTAL				$	$	
4.1 Legal, Admin, Bonding, Finance	%			$	$	%
V. PROJECT CONTINGENCY/ESCALATION	%			$	$	
VI. TOTAL PROJECT BUDGET				$	$	

Allowable Reimbursable Square Footage: sf
Adjustment for State "Allowable Square Footage Per Pupil" Calculation: %

To Be Paid By Town

of regional estimating experts in both general construction and mechanical and electrical trades to adjust the unit costs used in our estimates. Doing so allows us to be sensitive and responsive to the cost-control side of the design equation while still being able to develop highly creative and exciting solutions to a community's needs.

Success in cost control starts with the development and ongoing refinement of a realistic and comprehensive project budget. The Master Control Budget that we have developed not only lists a project's "Capital Construction Costs" but also includes "Other Capital Costs" (e.g., costs of land and equipment) and "soft costs" (for fees and expenses). (Examples of these kinds of costs include architectural and engineering fees, testing, special inspectors' fees, moving and storage, bid printing and advertising, renderings, models, computer-generated "fly-throughs," and construction management.) Building committees find this to be a valuable tool for continually evaluating and managing the total cost of their projects.

Like the detailed Task Schedule, the Master Control Budget is a dynamic document that tracks costs as work progresses and is further defined. This framework facilitates timely, proactive adjustments to keep the project within its budget guidelines. The sample Master Control Budget included here would, of course, be customized for a specific project.

Project Management: The Essential Components. Essential elements of Fletcher Thompson's project management process are summarized in the following lists:

Team Organization
- Entire team committed to design excellence
- Key team members participate throughout the process
- One point of contact is designated
- Proper staff allocation and consultant participation are ensured

Project Management
- Facilitate, record, and clarify team communications
- Define performance criteria and expectations
- Develop detailed Task Schedule with team
- Maintain all critical decision time frames

Cost Control
- Define scope of work commensurate with budget
- Maximize project value throughout the process
- Generate design and bid alternatives
- Develop and continually utilize Master Control Budget

Quality Assurance
- Define excellence as a goal
- Make continuous product improvement efforts

- Use accurate and up-to-date data
- Provide bimonthly peer reviews
- Strong construction administration resources
- Specify mock-up evaluations and standards

As must be very clear by now, collaboration—in planning, design, and construction—is a very complicated process. To make sure that everything that needs to be covered actually gets covered, thorough checklists are essential tools. Multifaceted, problem-solving discussions too often focus on one problem (or a limited set of problems), to the detriment of other agenda items that also require close attention—and there's no way to keep on track without checklists, which can themselves be refined and added to as the process proceeds. The checklists we provide in this chapter aren't meant to be complete or exhaustive, but to show you the range of areas and specific action items that such checklists might very well include.

Part III: The Elementary School of the Future

Chapter 8

The Elementary School of the Future:
Beliefs, Principles, and Goals

Fifty years ago, [public] school students graduated knowing perhaps 75 percent of what they would need to know to be successful in the workplace, family, and community. Today, the estimate is that graduates of our schools leave knowing perhaps 2 percent of what they will need to know in the years ahead—98 percent is yet to come. —Roland S. Barth (Barth, 2001)

Beliefs

The following basic beliefs were outlined by the Connecticut Association of Public School Superintendents' Technology Summit 2001 and published in a white paper issued by the group in January 2002 (Connecticut Association of Public School Superintendents, 2002):

Society has undergone a fundamental shift from an industrial economy to a knowledge economy. Schools based on the industrial model expect students to be compliant and dependent learners. In today's knowledge economy, students must be empowered to become self-directed, interdependent, and self-assessing learners. This shift requires a significant change in teaching and learning, and technology is a vital tool for accomplishing this shift.

To help students succeed in a knowledge economy,

- Educational leaders must establish a vision for this transformed view of teaching and learning, and they must model this transformation in their own learning and work experiences.
- Learners and their families must have equal access to tools that support their learning.
- The locus of control for learning must shift from teacher-directed to student-directed learning.
- Learners must master information literacy skills to access, investigate, and apply information.
- Learners must demonstrate their understandings and skills relative to measurable performance standards.

These basic beliefs should be supplemented by two others, taken from an article by educational facility designers Franklin Hill & Associates that appeared in the May/June 1998 issue of *The High School Magazine* (Franklin Hill & Associates, 1998):

- Schools that will thrive in the new millennium will find ways to contain their size while reducing their construction costs and increasing their efficiency and capacity.
- School facilities must evolve as a whole to support new teaching and learning paradigms. If we stubbornly cling to a systematic, incremental approach to change, our facilities will become a hodgepodge of unrelated elements that ultimately serve no coherent end.

Building Blocks for the General Principles

All discussion of educational specifications for the elementary school of the future must begin with an understanding of the General Principles. All requests for space and all future program development should be built upon them.

At the heart of the General Principles are three foundation blocks:

- Personalization
- Flexibility
- Technology

These three building blocks are at the base of all requests for space described in the Educational Specifications.

General Principles

To Build a Learning Community

- *Personalization.* The goal of the elementary school of the future should be to create an environment in which anonymity is banished. Every student will have an adult staff member, whether a homeroom teacher or a specialist, with whom she/he can talk on a regular and timely basis. With respect to class size, attention needs to be paid to keeping student/teacher ratios low.
- *Communication.* Spaces are needed where staff can converse with students, with each other, and with parents; where students can confer with other students; and where parents can meet and interact with other parents. Staff offices, student learning centers, shared workrooms, the student assembly/parent community room, the media center, and the student commons/cafeteria are spaces where such communication can occur.
- *Centers for student learning throughout the school.* No student should "fall through the cracks," and student learning centers are a major vehicle for achieving this goal. These areas will provide space where teachers can give academic support to all students, individually and in small groups, as well as venues for close teacher/student interaction.

To Build a Dynamic Curriculum to Enhance Student Learning

- Technology in every classroom.
- Classrooms that support diverse instructional strategies. Classrooms must be appropriately sized and shaped to enable teachers to work with an entire class of students, with groups of classes for special presentations, and with individual or small groups of students working together.
- Space for teachers to collaborate with each other. Shared workrooms and shared student learning centers will help to encourage discussions and planning, leading to greater collaboration.

To Promote Excellence in Student Achievement

- Quiet work areas for teachers and students.
- Library/media center for large- and small-group instruction and individual study.
- Technological resources for staff and students.
- Flexible classrooms large enough to accommodate large-group instruction and student-directed learning in small groups. Classrooms and hallways need to be flexibly designed so students can work individually or in small groups, or so that two classes can be grouped together. Every room, common area, and office will be wired for technology. Students in the elementary school of the future will all have age-appropriate wireless laptop computers that they will use in classrooms and elsewhere, doing research via the Internet. All teachers will have websites, and teachers will communicate directly with students and parents at home through email.

To Serve the Needs of Diverse Learners

- Learning areas that foster the use of a variety of instructional strategies that match the needs of individual learners. Students have unique strengths and weaknesses; they possess different and differing interests. The elementary school of the future must provide appropriate learning environments for all its students.
- Space for instructional and non-instructional student support services. The student cafeteria/commons area should provide space for students to relax and talk to teach other. The student assembly/parent community room should provide an area for student government activities, as well as a place where parents can discuss school and community concerns among themselves or with members of the staff. The more parents are aware of and involved in the activities of the school, the more effective the school becomes.

To Ensure Flexibility

- Classrooms and other learning areas must be able to be used in different ways to reflect changes in curriculum, technology, educational research, and/or board of education policy. We know that a dynamic curriculum responds to developments in educational research, to the demands of the community, to changes in board of education policy, and to changes in technology. The educational specifications are designed such that the building will accommodate a changing curriculum and changes in program or daily schedule.

To Promote a Comfortable and Healthy Environment

- An HVAC system that provides adequate heat, ventilation and air conditioning.
- Adequate storage space.
- Effective communication systems.
- Full compliance with the Americans with Disabilities Act (ADA), Occupational Safety and Health Administration (OSHA), and local fire

department requirements. To be effective, a facility must provide for the safety, health and comfort of its occupants.

Architectural Goals

According to the *Chicago Public Schools Design Competition, 2000/2001 Competition Program* (Chicago Public Schools, 2000/2001), designers should consider the following architectural goals as key to the design of the elementary school of the future:

- Architecture to maximize student independence.
- Spaces to foster integration and cooperation and encourage student interaction.
- Architecture to foster learning through an array of building materials.
- Environment to encourage interactive exploration and learning with a variety of mediums (such as plants, sand, etc.)
- Architecture with an inherent, understandable order. Confusing circulation paths and a complex building structure should be avoided.
- A non-institutional, child-centered learning environment.
- Environment with a variety of visual cues and other orientation aids.

Chapter 9

The Elementary School of the Future: A Draft Educational Specification

The elementary school of the future will increasingly provide space for family and community functions that used to take place in the home, the neighborhood, and the community in general. Family activities ranging from eating to exercising, from celebrating to decision-making will occur with regularity in the school facility. The school will be utilized for these functions on an 18/7/365 basis.

In tomorrow's schools, learning activities will be dispersed among many spaces, including (but not limited to) the classroom, the agora, and larger multipurpose facilities. In this scheme, it's helpful to think of these spaces as expanding networks of social interaction, with the classroom representing the home, the agora representing a neighborhood, and the larger multipurpose facilities representing the community as a whole.

The Classroom

The homeroom classroom, with its teacher-surrogate parent, will act as a home away from home. It will be the place, if you will, for retreat and reflection, for support and stimulation, and for renewal and encouragement. The homeroom teacher will work from a fully equipped cubby designed to enable the teacher to electronically access information from all available resources, including the student's personal file. The cubby will be spacious enough for student-teacher conferences or student-teacher-parent meetings. The classroom, minus storage and computers, could be smaller than the typical present-day classroom, with movable chairs and desks whose trapezoid-shaped tops will allow them to be merged into circular formations or separated for individual use. The desktop will accommodate a wireless laptop or personel digital assistant (PDA) plus keyboard, with room for reference papers and reading/writing activities.

Students will follow individualized educational prescriptions for learning in accordance with their own capacities and abilities primarily in the homeroom/classroom setting.

The classroom learning environment will be enhanced by a heating, ventilating, and air-conditioning system that does an excellent job of conditioning the air, by some windows that open, by an abundance of natural light, and by acoustically treated walls. All classrooms will be equipped with a sound-amplification system, with each teacher wearing a microphone so all students can hear at the same level.

The room will also have a ceiling mounted projection system, controlled from the teacher workstation, allowing for full, Internet-related audio/video access.

The Agora

The elementary school of the future will be arranged into "pods" organized by grade level, age level, and/or discipline level, depending on the school's choice. In each pod, or neighborhood, four or more classrooms will surround an all-purpose space accommodating approximately 150 students. Various names have been proposed for this all purpose space: *agora* (from the marketplace, or public forum, of ancient Greek cities, where teachers and students met to discuss ideas); *kiva* (from the community gathering place in the pueblos of the American Southwest); and *generative space*, because it's here that ideas, an understanding of group dynamics, and a sense of community are generated. The agora is a place for presentation, problem-solving, and participatory decision-making. The square feet saved by specifying smaller classrooms can be spent on the agora.

Multipurpose Facilities

Depending on the needs and size of the school, even larger groups of students or even the entire school community, including parents and friends, can be brought together in a cafetorium (combination cafeteria/auditorium), a gymnatorium (combination gymnasium/auditorium), or a multipurpose auditorium. This space is an extension of the community concept that is so important to the elementary school of the future. The larger agoras and the multipurpose auditorium/gymnasium/cafeteria spaces will be utilized for large-group learning.

Other Features

Beyond the features stipulated in the draft educational specification that appears below, we suggest that the following features be incorporated in the elementary school of the future:

- In the auditorium, flexible seating and partitions for small- and large-group instruction.
- A gymnasium equipped for full physical and sensory exploration, in accordance with district curriculum.
- Specialized science classrooms with space for laboratory experimentation, virtual learning, and presentation/discussion.
- A cafeteria capable of accommodating small-group meals, with vending machines for evening and early morning snacks, and with equipment for formal group presentations/discussions.
- A site that is developed and designed with an eye toward preserving and appreciating the environment. The site should include a quarter-mile walking track, a fish and reflecting pool, sandboxes, vegetable gardens, flower beds, bird-feeding stations, areas for meditation and reflection, and playing fields designed to serve users of all ages.
- Staff facilities including faculty lounges, vending machines for after-hours meals, and exercise and shower areas complete with adequate clothes lockers. Teachers need to be able to access and utilize the facility on an 18/7/365 basis.

Overview of the School

The design population for this school is 150 pre-K students and 500 students in grades pre-K through 5.

Classroom and program-area sizes given in this document include preliminary square footage estimates that may be revised during the final design process. We suggest that consideration be given to combining certain spaces' uses: for example, if the auditorium, cafeteria, or physical education spaces can do double duty as instructional spaces without compromising their main purposes—and thereby reduce the total number of square feet needed in the building—such design alternatives should be considered. Other proposed design solutions include the use of relatively soundproof movable dividers in some classroom areas and the addition of meeting areas—agoras, or kivas—in the classroom pods.

The entire building must be air conditioned and must meet the various applicable code requirements. Heating and air-conditioning equipment should be energy efficient, and environmental/sustainable building materials should be used in construction to the greatest extent possible. The building will be wired with fiber optic cable for current and future technology. Natural lighting will be maximized. Classrooms will be designed for flexible use.

The pre-kindergarten program will be provided with appropriately designed dedicated spaces. Children with disabilities will have the opportunity of learning and playing with other children of the same age. Pre-kindergarten children should be able to participate selectively in building-wide events, programs, and celebrations.

Each student will have an age-appropriate portable computer or PDA with wireless capabilities. Each teacher will have an office area, perhaps in the classroom, with a dockable laptop computer connected to a large monitor wired into the district's local area network. Classrooms will have ceiling-mounted computer projectors and speech-amplification systems. Students' portable computers will double as electronic readers that, eventually, will hold most reading materials. Space in classrooms and the library/media center that, today, is ordinarily allocated for book storage and stand-alone computers can be eliminated. Classroom furniture will be movable, and each desktop will have adequate space for a portable computer and writing materials. Each classroom will have an electronic workboard/smart board. Technology should include an appropriate infrastructure, including adequate data storage associated with a high-speed data transmittal system with school-home connectivity. Wireless cell phones should be used where possible.

Large-group spaces (gymnasium, cafeteria, auditorium) will be located so as to provide public access during non-school hours without compromising the security of the building. The entire facility will be fenced and lockable in accordance with district direction. Video surveillance cameras and appropriate alarm systems must be included. Fingerprint-reading locks or other biometric access-control devices and bar-code student activity and purchasing cards should also be utilized.

Detailed Descriptions of Instructional Spaces

Kindergarten/Grade One Classrooms
(Total: approximately 8,500 square feet)

There will be four kindergarten classrooms of 1,000 square feet each and five grade-one classrooms of 900 square feet each. The rooms will have tiled floors with carpeted areas; the carpet will be removable for cleaning. Each room will have its own unisex, disabled-accessible toilet facility for students. Each room will be equipped with teacher desk, chair, file cabinet, teacher's computer station, tack boards and dry-erasable boards, and storage and shelving for instructional equipment and materials. The following are also needed in each kindergarten and grade-one classroom: a disabled-accessible sink, cabinets, cubbies, and adjustable circular tables and student chairs. Lockers for children's clothing should be provided outside the rooms. The rooms will each have a printer, television, VCR/DVD player, microwave, globe, wardrobe, blocks, easels, and other age-appropriate learning materials.

Use of these rooms will be flexible, allowing each teacher to establish learning centers and to teach from any section of the room.

General Classrooms—Grades Two through Five
(Total: approximately 15,200 square feet)

There will be 16 classrooms for grades two through five. Twelve of these will be 900 square feet each; four classrooms will be 1,100 square feet each to accommodate science laboratory equipment for grades four and five. (An alternative, mentioned above, would be to have two or more specialized classrooms dedicated to science instruction only.) These rooms will have tiled floors. There will be adequate power outlets throughout the rooms. Each room will contain the following: teacher desk and chair, computer/printer station, television, VCR/DVD player, file cabinet, desks and chairs for 25 students, one round and one rectangular table with six chairs each, built-in bookshelves and storage cabinets, an electronic workboard, student lockers outside of classrooms, accessible sink with cabinetry, pull-down maps, globe, tack boards, and dry-erasable boards.

Library/Media Center
(Total: approximately 5,800 square feet)

The library/media center will be centrally located within the building and will include a computer lab and a world language lab. Every effort will be made to maximize sources of natural lighting. The entire area, with the exception of work areas, will be carpeted. It will be possible to lock the library/media center for security purposes. The main space within the library/media center will contain a two-level circulation desk with two computer stations and a printer, telephone, and storage and shelving behind the desk. A separate instructional area for 25 students with 8 rectangular tables and 35 chairs should be included. A carpeted story area, conducive to independent reading and with soft furniture and space to allow students to sit on the floor to listen to stories, will be included. The room will be equipped with whiteboards, bulletin boards, and display cases. A separate space for a professional library for teachers should also be included. The library will require 40 units of lower-height shelving to meet ADA standards. Additional items include 8 rectangular tables with 40 chairs, 1 television, 1 VCR/DVD player, 1 pull-down screen, 1 presentation station including computer, 10 online catalogue stations, teleconferencing equipment, and a kiosk for loading/unloading 100 electronic readers.

The library workroom will require racks, shelving, and carts for processing materials, storage cabinets, a counter and sink, a copier, a computer, a printer, and two desks.

The computer lab will house 25 computers, 3 printers, a scanner, and a network server. Cabling will be installed in the floor. The publishing/production/TV area will include a presentation station, a high-speed connection to the school's local area network for Internet access, a centralized data communication rack, and a centralized video distribution rack. An additional communication closet is needed to comply with electronics and telecommunications industry standards. The world language lab will require 25 computer stations with a main teaching station console and appropriate server.

Gymnasium
(Total: approximately 5,450 square feet)

The gymnasium will have a wooden floor with cushioned underlay. It should be located near a building entrance, but not at the front of the building or in the classroom area. It should offer easy access for after-hours activities. Toilet rooms should be located directly outside the gymnasium. Equipment for the gymnasium will include wall padding, an electronic score board, four retractable blackboards and two fixed backboards, retractable bleachers, volleyball stanchions, gymnastic equipment and pit, nets, and miscellaneous equipment. The equipment storage area should have storage racks and shelving. Gym office space will accommodate two teacher desks, chairs, file cabinets, a telephone, and a toilet room with sink. Windows to observe activity in the gymnasium should also be included.

Auditorium
(Total: approximately 9,700 square feet)

The school auditorium will provide a multifunctional instructional and performance facility for school programs and events that may be geared to varying groupings of the school's population. In addition, it will be used for school-wide events such as concerts, performances, spelling bees, math

Olympiads, and school-wide meetings, as well as for parent presentations and for public events sponsored by the town government and local community groups.

The auditorium will provide fixed seating for 500 and portable seating for 100 in a "pit" configuration and will be equipped with lighting, sound, and rigging systems appropriate to elementary school performances and presentations.

Music
(Total: approximately 2,240 square feet)

Two rooms are dedicated to the music program: the choral room will accommodate a full grade-level class of students; the instrumental room will serve smaller instrumental groups. The choral room will have a tiled floor with carpeted area in front. It will have acoustical treatment on the walls and power outlets in the floor. It will be equipped with a teacher desk/chair and podium, 125 stacking chairs, a television, a VCR/DVD player, a computer station with speakers, 20 electronic musical keyboards, disabled-accessible risers, storage cabinets with horizontal shelving, a dry-erasable board, tack boards, a piano, and a four-drawer lateral file cabinet. The instrumental room will be carpeted, have acoustical wall treatment, a computer station, 25 music stands, 50 stackable chairs, a lateral music storage file, a dry-erasable board, a tack board, a teacher desk/chair and podium, and shelving (both open and closed, with locks) for instruments. The music library/storage area (in between both rooms) should include practice rooms with glass observation panes and should have cabinets with horizontal shelves, a teacher's keyboard, a VCR/DVD player, a cart, a record/CD/tape player, and speakers. A sink should be available for instrument repair.

Art
(Total: approximately 1,600 square feet)

The fine arts room will be visited on a regularly scheduled weekly basis by all classes. This room will be equipped as follows: a teacher workstation with chair, a chalkboard, one wall of storage cabinets with corkboard panels in front and horizontal shelving, a high counter with vertical shelving, 10 computer stations equipped with specialized software including CD-burning capability, a color printer, a television monitor, a VCR/DVD player, 2 to 4 sinks (2 higher, 2 lower height), 6 student tables, 25 chairs, 2 drying racks, 2 easels, and a clay bin. Natural daylighting should be maximized in the room, and artificial lighting should be provided by rows of white fluorescent fixtures, with all the rows on separate switches, as well as spotlighting on a separate switch. Power outlets will be distributed along the walls. The room will have a tile floor. The ceramic room will be in an adjacent area separated by a window wall. It will contain an FA88 kiln with kiln timer and temperature gauge, a kiln vent, and wire storage racks. Display cases and bulletin boards should be outside the art room. The art storage room will have 32-inch-deep horizontal shelving, some vertical storage shelving, and a three-tiered metal cart.

Pre-Kindergarten Program
(Total: approximately 11,050 square feet)

The pre-kindergarten program will be connected to the kindergarten area in a separate wing of the building. The facility will have access to an outdoor area with appropriate playground equipment; a portion of the outdoor area should have a roof over it for protection from the sun. Both the kindergarten and pre-kindergarten areas will have appropriate enclosed changing areas. There will be eight pre-K classrooms, each with an exit to the outside. Each classroom will contain an area with two mini-toilets, sinks, and a "changing" counter. Each will have a one-way observation mirror to the hallway, a cabinet space for storage, a wall-mounted television, and a VCR/DVD player. Each room will have a tiled floor with a carpeted area. Also included will be 48-inch-high cubbies for student projects, two whiteboards, one tack board, clothing lockers for students, a dimmer control for the lighting, bookcases, five low student tables with 15 chairs, two easels, and sets of blocks and other age-appropriate instructional equipment. Additionally, there will be a counter with a sink, set in a cabinet with locking doors, and shelves and a mirror above the sink. There will be two computers in each classroom. Each room will contain a low drinking fountain.

The pre-kindergarten wing will provide office space for program leaders, specialists, and support staff. A PPT conference room is included in this area and will be furnished with an oval table and chairs to seat 12 to 14 people. Specifications for these areas are the same as those described for similar functions in the K-5 sections of the building. They include:

- Administrative offices
- Social worker's office
- Psychologist's office
- Speech/language room/office
- Nursing area

The OT/PT/motor skills room will contain two exposed beams for attachment of support harnesses for swings, wall hooks to hang six floor mats, a storage closet and cabinets, and a wall-hung mirror. It will be carpeted.

A kitchen/utility space within the pre-kindergarten area will contain a stove, refrigerator, microwave, sink, clothes washer/dryer, and storage cabinets.

Detailed Description of Support Facilities

School Administration
(Total: approximately 1,480 square feet)

The administrative area, located at the front of the building, will include offices for the principal and assistant, a general office area with reception space, a work/storage room, and a conference room. A Parent Teacher Association (PTA) room will be located adjacent to the administrative area.

The principal's and assistant's offices will each contain a desk, chair, computer, printer, telephone, bookshelf, and file cabinet. These offices will be carpeted and will have windows to the outside as well as one-way windows to the general office and corridor. Both offices will include a round conference table and chairs.

The general office/reception area will have a two-person workstation including desks, chairs, telephones, and computers. The office will contain teacher mailboxes, the building's intercom system, a fax machine, and a two-level counter. The reception area will be furnished with five waiting room-type chairs.

The work room will house a copy machine, lockable file cabinets for record storage, a safe, adequate counter space, and cabinets for storage.

The PTA room, adjacent to the administrative area, will have a round table, 10 chairs, a computer, a printer, a photocopying machine, a telephone, and shelving or closed cabinets.

The administrative conference room will have an oval table with chairs to seat 12. The conference room should be directly accessible from both the general office and the principal's office.

Coat closets must be provided for staff and visitors within the administrative area.

Adult toilet rooms will be located adjacent to the administrative area.

Resource Center
(Total: approximately 6,000 square feet)

The resource center will contain offices for special education resource teachers, the school psychologist, the social worker, the speech therapist, and the coordinator of the talented and gifted program. The literacy facilitator's and tutors' offices, the speech/language room, the reading recovery room, and the planning and placement team (PPT) conference room will located be in this area. The resource center offices and the conference room will be carpeted; classrooms and resource rooms will have tiled floors, with a carpeted area in the classroom.

The specialists' offices will each contain a desk, a chair, a small round table with four chairs, a file cabinet, bookcase, a telephone, a bulletin board, a computer with printer, and a dry erase board.

The three special education resource rooms will be in classroom areas. These will have computer stations, whiteboards, bulletin boards, bookcases, storage for instructional supplies, tape recorders, and two small round tables with four student chairs.

The literacy facilitator will have a separate office containing a desk, chair, file cabinets, a tack board and shelving; it will be carpeted. Adjacent to the facilitator's office will be a larger office to be shared by four tutors. The tutors' office will have desks and chairs, computer stations, file cabinets, and a storage area. An adjacent room will have four separate teaching areas equipped for flexible small-group instruction. Flexible wall partitions may be used. This room will have small rectangular tables, each with four student chairs; shelving for storage; file cabinets; dry-erasable boards; and tack boards.

The reading recovery room will be a small room with a large viewing window (one-way window). It will contain a teacher's work area and a large table and student chairs. Also included are storage cabinets and open horizontal shelving, a file cabinet, whiteboards, and tack boards.

The speech/language room/office will be carpeted, with acoustic tile on the ceiling. One wall will have a soft surface such as corkboard or feltboard. There will be an acoustical seal around the door of this room. The room will have a small, double-paned window. The room will contain an adjustable round table with six chairs; a teacher desk and chair; a child-size computer table, with computer; a locked storage closet; bookshelves; a mirror; and hearing and speech testing equipment.

The PPT conference room will be furnished with an oval table and chairs to accommodate 12 to 14 people.

Cafeteria/Kitchen
(Total: approximately 6,600 square feet)

The cafeteria will feed 190 students per seating. It will be treated with acoustical wall panels to dampen sound. It will be furnished with 15 telescoping round tables and 300 folding or stacking chairs. Colors and lighting will be selected to enhance the environment and to encourage students to unwind.

Careful attention will be given to the design of the serving area in order to create the most efficient traffic flow pattern and, if possible, to provide a separate faculty food line directly off the faculty room. The faculty dining room should contain two or three round tables with chairs, a sofa, and two easy chairs. A phone in a private area will be provided. An effort will be made to provide some separation between the dining and work areas of this room. The work area will contain a counter, cabinets, and a copy machine.

The kitchen will be designed and constructed in accordance with applicable guidelines and in adherence to health codes. There will be office space for the manager and locker/toilet space for the staff. The kitchen will be adjacent to the receiving area. All surfaces will be washable. The following will be included: a combined walk-in cooler/freezer; separate storage for food and cleaning supplies; separate sinks; fire extinguishers; one microwave oven; one double-stack convection oven; a two-compartment pressure steamer and a steam-jacketed kettle; a commercial stove with fire-suppression hood system; a computer and printer; food preparation tables including some with butcher-block surfaces; pots, pans, and other utensils; and serving counters for hot and cold food.

Nursing Area
(Total: approximately 510 square feet)

The school nurse will be housed close to the administrative area. Included in this space will be a small private office for the nurse containing a desk, chair, telephone, computer, two file cabinets, and a tiled floor. A disabled-accessible toilet and sink will be provided. The nurse's office will be separated from the student resting area by a glass window wall. The resting area will have four cots, privacy curtains, counter space, and locking cabinets for storage of medications and other supplies. There will be two sinks in this area, bright lights on a dimmer switch, a step-on trash can, a wheelchair, vision screening equipment, custom cabinets, and other miscellaneous medical equipment.

A similar nursing area will be created in the pre-kindergarten wing. It will be slightly smaller and will contain two cots.

Time-Out Room

A small room with a teacher's desk, cabinets, shelving, bulletin boards, and two round tables with four student chairs will be used as a time-out room for children.

Family Resource Center
(Total: approximately 1,900 square feet)

One room of 1,200 square feet, with tiled floors and carpeted areas, will serve as the family resource center. The room will be flexibly equipped to allow the creation of learning centers or to support large-group activities. The room will be equipped with tack boards and dry-erasable boards, as well as storage and shelving for instructional equipment and materials. Also needed in this area are a disabled-accessible sink with cabinets and adjustable rectangular/circular tables with student chairs for pre-schoolers. A disabled-accessible toilet for students should also be available. The room should also have an area for coats.

A separate conference room/parent resource room of 400 square feet should be adjacent to the main room. This room should have adult toilet facilities. It should be carpeted and have appropriate shelving for storage of resources. Five soft chairs and a rectangular table with chairs for 10 to 12 should also be included.

An office of 300 square feet for the director and her staff will contain two desks, chairs, a small round table with four chairs, file cabinets, bulletin boards, and dry-erasable boards. A computer with a printer should also be available.

Chapter 10

**The Elementary School
of the Future:
Conceptual Drawings**

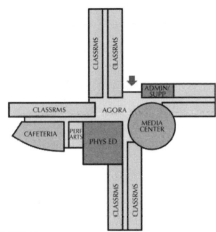

LINEAR PINWHEEL

- Discontinuity of classroom areas limits grade flexibility
- Dead-end circulation
- Easily expanded classroom areas
- Difficult expansion of core areas
- Site intensive footprint

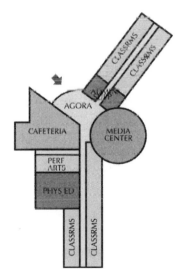

LINEAR CHEVRON

- Discontinuity of classroom areas limits grade flexibility
- Dead-end circulation
- Easily expanded classroom areas
- Difficult expansion of core areas
- Simple, clear organization

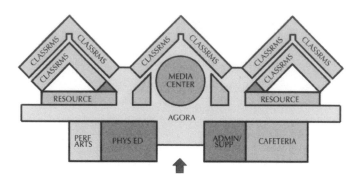

LINEAR CLUSTER

- Subdivision of classroom areas creates more intimate scale
- Hierarchical circulation allows a variety of experiences
- Good separation of public and private
- Easily expanded classroom areas
- Easily expanded core areas

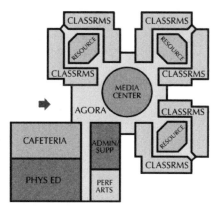

ACADEMIC CLUSTER

- Discontinuity of classroom areas limits grade flexibility
- Subdivision of classroom areas creates more intimate scale
- Difficult expansion of classrooms
- Good separation of public and private
- Loop circulation eases congestion
- Compact footprint

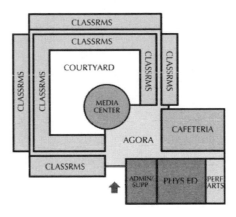

COURT/CORE

- Continuity of classroom areas allows good grade flexibility
- Good separation of public and private
- Loop circulation eases congestion
- Compact footprint
- Easily expanded core areas
- Easily expanded classroom areas

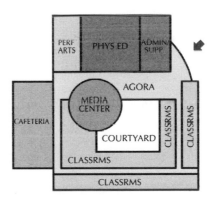

COMPACT COURT

- Continuity of classroom areas allows good grade flexibility
- Loop circulation eases congestion
- Compact footprint
- Easily expanded core areas
- Easily expanded classroom areas

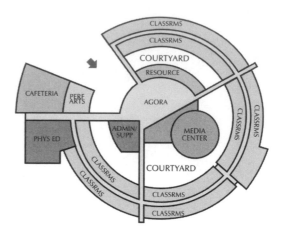

COURT/CENTRAL PAVILLION

- Continuity of classroom areas allows good grade flexibility
- Loop circulation eases congestion
- Good separation of public and private
- Difficult expansion of classrooms
- Difficult expansion of core areas

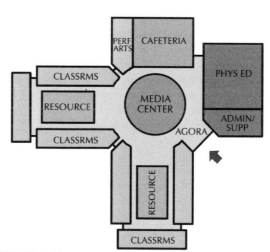

CENTERED HOUSE PLAN

- Subdivision of classroom areas creates more intimate scale
- Discontinuity of classroom areas limits grade flexibility
- Difficult expansion of classrooms
- Loop circulation eases congestion
- Difficult expansion of core areas

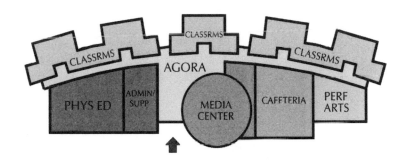

LINEAR MAIN STREET

- Subdivision of classroom areas creates more intimate scale
- Continuity of classroom areas allows good grade flexibility
- Simple, clear organization
- Good separation of public and private
- Dead-end circulation

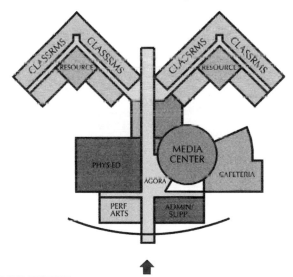

LINEAR/CLUSTER

- Hierarchical circulation allows a variety of experiences
- Subdivision of classroom areas creates more intimate scale
- Discontinuity of classroom areas limits grade flexibility
- Difficult expansion of classrooms
- Good separation of public and private
- Dead-end circulation

Part IV: Issues in Elementary School Planning, Design, and Construction

Chapter 11

Site Design and Landscape Architecture for the Future Elementary School

by Barry Blades, ASLA

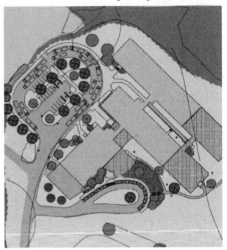

Like so many other aspects of school planning and design, the process of locating a site for a new school, designing that site, and providing an appropriate landscape architectural treatment has grown much more complicated over the past two decades or so. Today, landscape architects designing and landscaping the grounds of a typical elementary school must respond to a very broad range of sometimes-conflicting needs, regulations, and contingencies, the most important of which are discussed below. What will the future bring? That, of course, is always hard to say. But extrapolating from current trends, it is likely that the many forces now affecting the siting and landscaping of our schools will intensify and that their interaction will become even more complex in the years to come.

The Automobile

Americans love their cars. There's nothing new in that, but what we have noticed in recent years is an increasing tendency for elementary school children to be taken to and from school by private car. Many parents seem to have gotten in the habit of picking their children up from school for after-school activities and this, in turn, appears to have encouraged them to start bringing their kids to school by car, as well.

At suburban elementary schools these days, it's not unusual to see a significant number of parents waiting in their cars for their children at the end of the school day. And, in trying to reach spots near the school's doors, parents' vehicles frequently come into conflict with buses. Though mornings are generally less problematic (everyone doesn't arrive at once, and there's no waiting around), the traffic congestion caused by private-car drop-offs can still be significant. Designers are having to accommodate this trend— that is, to develop strategies for relieving the congestion and lessening the conflict—in their designs for new elementary school sites.

Additionally, although parking space is always at a premium on new school sites, the challenge of providing adequate parking has been exacerbated recently because of the increasing after-hours use of elementary school buildings by the wider community. It's seldom, if ever, possible to provide all the parking space needed for after-hours users (or for visitors attending a special event), but designers try to accommodate such needs in their plans—for instance, by earmarking lawns, paved play areas, and/or athletic fields for occasional drive-up parking, by identifying convenient off-site parking areas (in nearby parks or around nearby churches), or by designing paved areas that are used infrequently (e.g., bus queue lanes, maintenance roads, etc.) and that can serve as overflow, special-event parking.

Beyond the adequacy of parking space, the issue of convenient accessibility of parking areas to school entrances has also become more problematic than in the past. Today, security concerns (to which we return, below) encourage administrators at many schools to maintain only one open entrance during the normal school day. Typically, both parent queuing and visitor parking areas are located near this entrance so that administrators can properly monitor the flow of these occasional users. Because of the lack of available space, the bus loop and faculty parking are then located to access other building entrances that can be locked down after the morning arrival and afternoon departure times. Even on a relatively large site, therefore, it's likely that some parking areas will be rather far from the entrance. When coupled with accessibility requirements mandated by the Americans with Disabilities Act (ADA) and other, similar laws and regulations (a subject we also return to, below), this can pose some thorny challenges to landscape architects.

Site Conditions

Relatively large sites are, of course, increasingly rare commodities. U.S. suburbs are overbuilt, and the competition for desirable land for other uses (residential, commercial, etc.) is tremendous. Thus, there are fewer and fewer "perfect" sites on which to place a new school. Elsewhere in this book (see chapter 2, "Cost, Change, and School Construction"), mention is made of the impact that this situation is having on first costs because of the stepped-up need, in so many cases, to perform extensive site remediation (e.g., grading, rock excavation, etc.) before construction can begin. But the shortage of suitable sites is causing other side-effects, as well.

Among these are the site-design challenges that emerge when new-school sites are in close proximity to neighbors. Twenty years ago, a new school building could be plunked down in the middle of fields or a forested area, and designers did not typically need to be overly concerned with the school's impact on distant residential or commercial properties. Now, noisy, smelly, or "messy" areas—school bus queuing areas, playgrounds and athletic fields, and service areas with garbage-disposal facilities (which have grown larger because of recycling regulations mandating a number of dumpsters or bins for different kinds of waste)—must often be carefully screened so as not to cause consternation to nearby homeowners and businesses.

Situating schools in developed neighborhoods can cause yet another quandary for landscape architects. Zoning regulations and a community's desire to maintain a consistent neighborhood landscape aesthetic often necessitate extensive landscaping at school sites. Unfortunately, the operating budgets of many schools are inadequate for the level of maintenance such landscaping requires. The design challenge, then, is to successfully blend the school's landscape into the fabric of the neighborhood without putting a burden on operating budgets.

The shortage of suitable sites also means that there are few new-school sites today that do not contain environmentally sensitive areas within their boundaries. In the Northeast, this most often entails wetlands areas that are protected by federal, state, and municipal regulatory agencies. To obtain permits from these agencies for activities that might impact the wetlands, it is often necessary to develop strategies for wetland "mitigation" that will compensate for the loss of wetland functional value. This mitigation can take a number of forms: for example, the cleanup of degraded wetland areas, the introduction of new landscaping that will provide food and habitat for wildlife, or the creation of new areas that provide wetland value. One form of mitigation that has been well received by regulatory agencies is the use of wetland areas as outdoor classrooms for schoolchildren studying biology, ecology, and botany.

But there are additional considerations when a school site contains environmentally sensitive zones: in some cases, wetlands and bodies of standing water must be fenced off for safety reasons. In almost all cases, stormwater management strategies (for example, biofilter pools and onsite detention basins) must be implemented to protect adjacent downstream properties. While wetlands and other bodies of standing water can be environmentally beneficial, they can also cause problems. If not properly designed and/or controlled, they can become breeding areas for mosquitoes—raising health concerns associated with these insects. Pesticides used for mosquito control can also cause concern.

Community Use

At the same time that school sites have been getting tighter (smaller, more constrained by environmental regulations and by the concerns of close-by neighbors), the demands placed on these sites have been growing. Elsewhere in this book, much is made of the trend toward after-hours use of elementary school buildings by the wider community. What's true indoors is true outdoors, as well. Just as elementary school auditoriums are increasingly playing host to local theater groups, town hall-type community meetings, and so on, elementary school grounds are doing double-duty: as play areas for children during the school day and as the venue for organized sports (both children's and adults') when school is not in session. Gone are the days when a typical suburban elementary school was surrounded by an informal lawn (and little else). Today, it's pretty much expected that a new school's site will include regulation- or near-regulation-size playing fields for a variety of sports (or fields that can easily be converted, on a seasonal basis, from one sport to another—baseball to soccer, for example). Some new elementary schools' sites also include walking/running tracks intended for use not just by the school's phys ed program but also, during off-hours and non-school days, by adult joggers and even for charity fundraising walkathons.

There's no question that greater use of school grounds by the surrounding community is a good thing—it enables the fuller use of resources that, in fact, belong to the entire community and it plays a major role in helping develop taxpayer/voter support for a school construction project. But it can magnify the challenges faced by site designers. As flat, easily developed land has become scarce, towns have sometimes had to choose sites with more significant topographic changes. These steeply sloping sites often require the terracing of amenities such as parking and athletic fields to minimize construction cost. Unfortunately, this terracing makes it more difficult to accommodate athletic fields, which sometimes have to be overlapped because of area limitations. Also, ADA-required accessibility to these fields can be more difficult to achieve.

Accessibility

The interplay of the various forces affecting site design can be seen from the fact that issues related to ADA-mandated accessibility by physical disabled people have already been mentioned twice: once in the context of parking and security concerns, and again in the context of the placement and design of athletic fields. Accessibility regulations have, unsurprisingly, also had significant effects on the design of school playgrounds (now more often referred to as "play stations" or "playscapes").

One such effect involves the material used for surfacing play areas. Options are limited, because the surfacing material has to meet two, potentially conflicting standards: it must be soft and resilient enough to minimize the potential for serious injury should a child fall while playing (in the trade, this is called "impact attenuation"), but it also must be firm enough to allow access to the play station by a wheelchair-bound child. Only a few materials—shredded wood fibers and synthetic rubber padding (either poured in place or in the form of pre-manufactured tiles)—can conform to both these standards. Thus, almost all play areas designed today utilize one of these two materials.

The ADA doesn't only cover accessibility, however. It mandates that real efforts be made to provide physically challenged people—including schoolchildren—with opportunities and experiences that are reasonably similar to those enjoyed by others. This, too, is influencing the design and use of play equipment. For example, sandboxes at grade level are being supplemented with sandboxes on raised platforms (which can be reached by wheelchair-bound kids). Specially designed swings, climbing structures, and other play apparatus are becoming standard equipment on school sites.

Safety And Security

Because each site presents a different set of challenges and opportunities, and because each town's building program and educational specifications differ from those of other towns, the site design for a school will always be unique to that site. One area where that's not true is playscape design: the overriding focus on children's safety has all but eliminated the architect-designed playgrounds of the past. Today, playscape equipment is manufactured by a few vendors who subject their products to rigorous testing to minimize the risk of injury to the children who will play on it.

Concern for schoolkids' safety and security affects site design in other, broader ways. For example, fencing is used much more liberally on the grounds of today's elementary schools than it was in the past, and at many schools' play areas, especially for children in the earliest primary grades, are enclosed, or partly enclosed, by wings of the school building—a sort of courtyard arrangement. (The John Trumbull Primary School, in Watertown, Connecticut, discussed in chapter 3, provides a good example of this strategy.)

Fenced or walled-off play areas serve two security-related purposes: they prevent children from, for example, running into streets or other unsafe areas when chasing after balls, but, by restricting children to areas where they can easily be seen and supervised, they also decrease the possibility that children might be led away by a noncustodial parent or other unauthorized individual.

At urban schools, security is aided by so-called "passive" site design. The principle's a simple one: avoid the potential for trouble by not creating spaces where trouble might develop. Building exteriors are free of nooks and crannies that could serve as hiding places; plantings are either minimal, so as not to provide places to lurk, or are composed of what is sometimes called "hostile shrubbery"—that is, thorny bushes that would make very unpleasant hideouts. The goal, obviously, is to maximize the ability to easily surveil the entire exterior. In suburban settings, that same principle mandates, where possible, that a school building be surrounded by a ring road that enables 24-hour surveillance by police and that gives unrestricted access to fire department and other emergency vehicles in the event of an emergency.

I've already talked about the way in which the concern for security—by restricting access to a single point of entry, often fairly far removed from parking areas—can sometimes create problems for the site designer. Controlling access by funneling all foot-traffic through a single entrance/exit more or less dictates that certain components of the site design—the bus queuing area, for example—be located directly adjacent to that entrance.

So far, most elementary schools are making only limited use of surveillance by closed-circuit television (CCTV) cameras. (The use of CCTV and other electronic surveillance and access equipment is much more common, and sophisticated, at the high school level.) Some elementary schools are placing such cameras at their front doors and perhaps at a few locations scattered around the grounds. And concern for safety and security has led to an increase of outdoor lighting (also necessary for CCTV) on elementary school sites. Outdoor lighting, however, once again raises the issue of the school's impact on adjacent residential properties.

Maintenance

Finally, we'd be irresponsible if we didn't return, at least briefly, to the impact of maintenance budgets on landscaping. (We've already mentioned the fact that community-enforced landscaping standards can create a dilemma for the landscape architect who wants to make sure that ongoing maintenance doesn't outstrip a school's operating budget.)

Funds earmarked for groundskeeping and gardening are—as every public school administrator is well aware—extremely limited, and those budgets are getting more pinched all the time. (The expense of cultivating flowerbeds that change from spring to summer to fall is simply too hard to justify in an era when districts are scrambling to find ways of reducing the number of children per class, raising teacher's pay, etc.) Today, landscape designers who work on schools tend to cast a microscopic eye even on such issues as whether a particular patch of lawn can be mowed by a large-width riding mower or requires a hand-mower. Decisions regarding whether to plant ever-green or deciduous bushes and trees and whether to use grass lawns or some other sort of ground-cover in certain locations (especially courtyards) are also dependent on the long-term maintenance costs of the various alternatives.

Similarly, while no one denies that wood site furniture looks and feels terrific, few districts have the money to spare for the periodic sanding and refinishing that's needed to keep wooden furniture in presentable shape. From a design point of view, the situation is made more palatable by the fact that much of the new outdoor furniture that's being made from recycled plastics and other high-tech materials is not only durable but looks pretty good, too. Cognizant of the limitations of operating budgets, designers are encouraging building committees to consider more durable materials that may have a higher up-front cost (e.g., concrete curbing, which is more resistant to damage from snow plows than is bituminous curbing) but that will reduce maintenance costs down the road.

As we said at the start of this chapter, it is reasonable to assume that the future of landscape design for elementary schools can be extrapolated from current trends. As suitable sites become even fewer, as environmental and accessibility regulations remain in force or intensify, as community use of school grounds expands, as concerns for children's safety and security heighten, and—assuming that the nation's oil supply remains unthreatened and Americans' love affair with their cars undiminished—as schools' need to accommodate private automobile traffic grows, site designers' and landscape architects' task will become ever more complex. Solutions will, undoubtedly, be found, even to the most difficult challenges. But arriving at those solutions will be a much smoother process if decision-makers understand all the forces at work, and the way they interact.

Chapter 12

Improving School Acoustics— A Systems Approach

Try reading the following paragraph:

> Many educators feel is important to acoustics in classrooms by children with problems but unnecessary do so in used by students normal hearing. Yet populations of students normal hearing also from better classroom.

Difficult (or impossible) to understand, yes? Why? Because every fourth word—or 25 percent of the text—has been removed. That's the visual equivalent of a *speech intelligibility rating of 75 percent*, which the Acoustical Society of America says is the acoustical condition that prevails in many American classrooms today (Seep et al., 2000). A look at this unintelligible paragraph makes it easy to understand that there is a direct correlation between speech intelligibility and student performance.

What the paragraph above means to say is:

> Many educators feel it is important to improve acoustics in classrooms used by children with hearing problems but unnecessary to do so in those used by students with normal hearing. Yet many populations of students with normal hearing also benefit from better classroom acoustics (Seep et al., 2000)

Adding the ten missing words back in makes a clear and concise statement—demonstrating quite neatly the critical importance of speech intelligibility and the meaninglessness of a statement not fully communicated. Granted, there are other clues to understanding the spoken word, such as body language, gestures, lip movement, voice modulation, and so on. These clues are most effective in a live, in-person presentation, but today's instructional methods include many prerecorded presentations as well as live distance-learning interactions, and these and other high-tech instructional modes will come into even greater use over the years to come. A 75 percent intelligibility rating in the classroom of the future is therefore unacceptable, especially when one considers that raising the level of intelligibility is, with some thoughtful planning and design, a fairly simple matter.

Why Does the Problem Persist?

One of the major reasons behind the poor acoustics in today's classrooms is a simple lack of awareness of the problem—this despite a recent U.S. General Accounting Office (GAO) report that ranks noisy classrooms high on the list of educators' frustrations. Poor acoustics is not a glaringly obvious problem; it cannot be recognized by simply walking into a room. Only the users of the space can discern it, and then only when actively engaged in the educational process. The GAO's *Condition of America's Schools, February 1995* survey reports that more than 28 percent of schools have unsatisfactory or very unsatisfactory acoustics for noise control (GAO,

1995). That's worse than the results for other environmental problems, including those involving ventilation, security, indoor air quality, heating, and lighting.

Given the total school-age population in the United States (47,200,000 pupils in 1999), this means that poor acoustics affect the learning process of millions of American students. And, unfortunately, the ill effects of poor speech intelligibility fall disproportionately on those who can least afford them. Overcrowding has a negative effect on classroom acoustics—and overcrowding is much more likely to occur in large urban schools and in schools that serve minority populations (Lewis et al., 1999). These are the same schools, of course, whose populations are most likely to include a high percentage of students for whom English is not their native language—and whose learning and performance are likely to suffer most from poor speech intelligibility.

Designs for elementary school classrooms still largely ignore the problem of classroom acoustics. New classrooms typically include acoustical treatments such as some carpet on the floor, acoustical tiles on the ceiling, gypsum wallboard partitions, and some batt insulation in the wall cavity between classrooms. Classrooms are also usually acoustically separated from adjacent spaces, but this typically represents the extent of acoustical design. Little, if any, consideration is given to specific acoustical criteria such as speech levels, background noise, reverberation times, or speech-to-noise ratios. And classrooms are typically designed repetitively: if there are no user complaints, the design is considered good, and so the next school project is designed in the same way the last school was. This method, however, ignores an important psychological reality—that users of a new facility are usually so gladdened by the opportunity to teach in brand new classrooms that they are hesitant to complain about "trivialities" such as classroom acoustics. After all, the thinking goes, the building was designed by experts. Assured that they have state-of-the-art classrooms, teachers remain unaware that classrooms might be even better, acoustically speaking.

The problem persists for a few other reasons, as well. One is that, until very recently, there have been no acoustical performance and testing standards for classrooms, so designers have had limited data on which to base their designs. A building code change, proposed to the International Code Commission (ICC) on November 14, 2001, adds a classroom acoustics section to the International Building Code (IBC). The proposed IBC is closely based on a draft ANSI standard (S12.60-20X). With ICC approval, classroom acoustic provisions become requirements in all states adopting the IBC. Obviously, every school design is unique, and each school has different programmatic needs, but careful use of guidelines and well-considered planning of all the spaces should go a long way toward solving the technical acoustical problems that are now so widespread.

Another reason for the problem's persistence has to do with the perceived cost of specialized design for acoustics or of remediating existing problems. But these costs should be considered as *integral* to the unit costs of a new building or renovation, and acoustical design should not be subject to value-engineering cuts. The value of acoustical improvements becomes clear when one considers that initial costs are far outweighed by the long-term costs resulting from disadvantaged learning.

Poor Speech Intelligibility—Origins of the Problem

Speech intelligibility can be impaired either by unintentional noise or by intentional sound that, for one reason or another, is inadequate to convey meaning effectively or that interferes with other intentional sound.

Unintended Noise. Background noise from an unintended source can compete with desired or intended sounds. Most commonly, background noise arises from building systems or from a lack of acoustical separation between occupied spaces. Here are some sources of the unintended noise that commonly afflicts school buildings.

- *Mechanical systems.* The need for ventilation and temperature control in modern schools requires that a large volume of air be constantly moved in and out of classrooms. That movement—the rush of air through ducts, grilles, and diffusers—can create background noise, which is often compounded by sounds generated by the fans and motors used to drive the air. In some older school buildings, steam heat—the hissing radiators and the banging pipes—contributes to the problem during the heating season. Classrooms located directly below the roof are subject to low-frequency vibrations created by rooftop-mounted mechanical equipment such as air-handling units, chillers, and exhaust fans.
- *Lighting and electrical systems.* Because of its economy and efficiency, fluorescent lighting has become the standard for virtually all buildings except residences. This type of lighting requires electronic ballasts, and these ballasts create a distinct hum. Electrical transformers that step down voltage, usually located in electric closets throughout a building, also emit a constant hum. Even though this noise is of a fairly low frequency and volume, it nonetheless contributes to background noise in adjacent areas. (Electrical switchgear also creates a hum, but this equipment is generally located well away from instructional spaces and contained in fire-rated spaces whose walls, coincidentally, acoustically isolate those spaces.)
- *People.* Background noise often results from people carrying on their everyday activities—moving around, talking, interacting, working. One often hears teachers complain about the noise created by the shuffling of desks and chairs. (And, in rooms with tile floors, one frequently finds an ad hoc solution to this problem: tennis balls stuck on the feet of desk and chair legs.) Other occupant-generated noise is an acoustical separation problem. Any movement through corridors outside the classroom (not to mention the banging of lockers) generates noise.

Sounds bleeding out into the corridor from classrooms whose doors have been left open to improve ventilation infiltrate nearby spaces. Food service areas can be particularly troublesome, acoustically. The movement and conversations of workers, product deliveries, and the ordinary use of utensils and equipment in the food-preparation process can, together, produce quite a racket. Though kitchen areas are typically back-of-the-house spaces, the noise can easily carry through reverberant corridors, as can the din produced in the cafeteria at mealtimes. Crossover noise emanating from gymnasiums or caused by custodial activities can, especially when combined with sounds from other sources, create a significant background noise level.

- *Reverberation.* Large spaces (cafeterias, gyms) are generally noisy spaces—not by planning but by default. Ask any teacher who's assigned lunch duty about the din in the cafeteria. These spaces are outfitted (appropriately) with washable surfaces that are hard and smooth—exactly the kind of surfaces that reflect sound. In such a space, reverberation time is extended, and sound is constantly being regenerated to produce a very high, constant background-noise level—the din. Too often, the cost of providing acoustical treatment to control such noise is perceived as prohibitive. If a gymnasium is noisy—so the thinking goes—that's okay because, after all, the gym is meant to house noisy activities. A gymnasium, however, isn't just a basketball/volleyball court with bleachers; it's also an instructional space, and the fact that physical education teachers, like all teachers, need to communicate information verbally should be considered when designing a gym.

- *Exterior noise.* Noises from the surrounding area—from vehicular or pedestrian traffic, from nearby manufacturing facilities or construction sites, or from lawnmowers and other onsite noise-generators—can infiltrate the school building. The sounds of children at play (especially in elementary schools, where outdoor play areas are generally located immediately adjacent or very close to the building) and of school buses queuing up for the afternoon trip home occur each and every school day.

Intentional Sounds. Sometimes intelligibility problems are created by the desired sound source itself. For example, if the sound source is weak it may not be able to overcome background noises such as those described above. Here are some of the intelligibility problems related to intended, rather than unintentionally produced, sounds.

- *Teachers' voices.* Obviously, every individual has a different voice pattern. Some people project well, with plenty of volume and good, clear articulation, while others are much more soft-spoken (with an endless range in between). Some teachers have speech impairment issues; others have foreign or regional accents that may make it difficult for the children they teach to understand them. And, of course, everyone occasionally suffers from an illness—a cold, sore throat, or laryngitis—that affects his or her speech. Those teachers who have difficulty overcoming background noise levels are those who suffer the most from poor acoustics. They must strain to be heard, which may color their presentation of the material and cause them unnecessary stress—perhaps even putting them at risk for stress-related health problems.

- *Audiovisual sound systems.* The A/V equipment used in schools is sometimes not as good—or in as good repair—as it might be. Intelligibility problems can occur if, say, the speaker system in a video monitor used for presenting a prerecorded program is inadequate or damaged, or if the equipment used in a live distance-learning is malfunctioning. In fact, if a video system is not a state-of-the-art product designed specifically for the space, then it can be reasonably assumed that it will be inadequate. Certainly, we've come a long way from the shaky-voiced, 16mm instructional movies of yesteryear, and vast improvements have been made in the content and production values of audiovisual presentations. But sound quality can still be a problem, and designers still struggle with the question of how best to distribute a clear and properly attenuated signal to each and every individual, especially in spaces where seating is not fixed. Turning up the volume only leads to greater distortion of the signal, and intelligibility does not necessarily improve. In fact, high-volume sound may bleed into other spaces—adding to the background noise level and disrupting activities in adjacent classrooms.

- *Public address sound systems.* Schools are required to have public address systems as part of a their emergency response plan. PA systems are also great communication tools for disseminating broadcast messages. Unfortunately, PA systems are subject to cost-cutting: good systems are value-engineered away, replaced with systems whose capabilities barely reach the minimum required for code compliance. For the most part, such systems produce poor quality, almost unintelligible sound.

- *Learning activities.* The clatter of a keyboard and the whirl of fans in a computer lab, the chatter of students working in small groups—these can also create background noise. When a student group is large or there are multiple small groups, the conversations will blend together, magnifying the problem.

- *Music and performing arts activities.* The construction budgets for many new elementary schools are not large enough to permit purpose-built auditoriums, which means that the gym or cafeteria must do double-duty as the venue for performances and large-group assemblies. But if you've ever attended a school band concert in a gymnasium you probably understand what bad acoustics are. Most gymnasiums simply don't work well as performance halls. (Schools that do have the funds to build an auditorium usually build it correctly—meaning that an expert in acoustics is consulted during design. Auditoriums are generally acoustically separated from surrounding spaces and do not present crossover acoustical problems.)

When background sound levels—whether produced by unintentional or intentionally produced sound—approach the level of the intended sounds in a classroom or other learning space, the message gets partially masked, resulting in a poor intelligibility rating.

The Systems Approach to Acoustical Design

The solution to poor speech intelligibility resides in a *systems approach* to acoustical design. Two basic principles underlie the systems approach:

1. *People, the users and occupants of the building, are an integral part of the system: they are often the generators of the sounds, and they are always the receptors of the sounds.* This means that decision-makers must be convinced of the importance of good acoustical design—that appropriate acoustical design carries a positive cost/benefit ratio. Student performance will be enhanced by the proper acoustical design of instructional spaces. The stress that teachers feel will diminish, and there will be a corollary reduction in stress-related health problems.

2. *All of a building's problems are in some way related to each another, so addressing only one problem without considering the overall system may well cause or exacerbate another problem.* An acoustical problem may be solved by adding a soft surface to a room, but that "solution" might provide an environment for mold growth. (This can cause problems not only for that space, but—because the mold spores can be distributed via the ventilation system—for the whole building.) Turning up the volume in one room may cause additional background noise in an adjacent room because of noise crossover through the adjoining ventilation-system ductwork; adding duct liners to reduce the crossover noise might, in turn, cause indoor air quality problems.

Some Design Guidelines

The following guidelines exemplify the systems approach.

Programming. In the programming phase, the acoustically critical spaces—particularly the core teaching/learning spaces—must be identified, and adjacency criteria must be established for them. In grades K-5 most students spend most of their time in a single classroom. If this room has acoustical problems, the students' ability to learn will be impaired. Adjacency studies should be part of the programming task. These matrix-type studies have long been part of the programming phase of all kinds of projects, but as the design profession has become increasingly specialized many programming tasks have become "second nature" and thus no longer received the focused attention they once did. To ensure good building acoustics, acoustical adjacencies should be carefully considered. Such studies will reveal problem areas that need special attention or treatment, as well as non-problematic areas that can be ignored.

Site Selection. The design process begins with site selection. In choosing a site for a new elementary school, diligent consideration should be given to the surrounding area, to identify both noise generators and sensitive receptors (because the school itself will be a noise generator). If at all possible, schools should be located far away from the following noise generators: manufacturing and industrial processing plants, warehouses/shipping facilities, retail facilities with frequent deliveries, landfills, emergency-vehicle stations (such as police, fire and ambulance stations), and municipal public works yards. Also to be avoided are sites near construction company yards where equipment is stored, and sites that are close to other sites where construction is scheduled or likely to occur. (Construction noise is, of course temporary, but keep in mind that construction on major projects can last for years.) Sites that are close to transportation infrastructure—railroads, light rail systems, airports, heliports, and highways (especially limited-access roads or major truck routes)—should be avoided. It's worth noting that many of the noise-generators listed here could also have a deleterious effect on other aspects of the school environment, as well—for example, vehicular exhaust from a nearby highway might have a negative impact on air quality inside and outside the school.

Site Design. Site designers need to consider the acoustical impact of areas where buses will queue and where parents will wait in their cars (with their motors running) to pick their children up from school. When deciding on the location of outdoor activity areas (playspaces, athletic fields, etc.), consideration should be given to how sound from those areas may affect activities within the building. Instructional areas inside the building should be located away from loading docks (which may have frequent truck traffic) and receiving areas.

Building and Classroom Design. All spaces in the building—but especially instructional spaces—should be designed to specific criteria in order to enhance those spaces' acoustical properties. The classroom is the core space of the educational process. All other spaces should therefore be designed around—and in deference to and support of—the classrooms. While design generally proceeds from the macro to the micro, classroom acoustics need to be considered early on as part of the overall building program to ensure that classrooms are acoustically efficient.

While there are multiple criteria for measuring and analyzing sound and the acoustical performance of spaces, most are too esoteric to be of practical value to educators. There are three acoustical criteria, however, that the decision-makers involved in school construction projects need to be aware of:

- Speech sound level
- Speech-to-noise (or signal-to-noise) and speech-to-reverberation ratios (S/N and S/R ratios)
- Reverberation time

These criteria are all expressed in terms of decibels (dB)—a measurement of sound pressure. The suffix "A" denotes the bandwidth of the measurement that closely approximates the normal range of human hearing. Reverberation time is measured in the number of seconds it takes for the reverberant sound to decay (or fade out) by 60 decibels. The criteria are as follows:

Speech sound level = 65dB(A) at all points in the room. This level can be attained through normal speech without amplification in a regular classroom with some acoustical treatments, such as acoustical ceilings and carpet on the floor.

S/N and S/R ratios = +15 dB(A) at all points in the room (background noise levels not to exceed 35 dB(A) as measured in an unoccupied room). This is a comparison of the desired sound to the background noise Speech/Noise ratios (S/N ratios) express the difference between the sound levels of the speech and the noise. Since both the speech and noise are measured in dB(A), the S/N ratio, a relative measure, is simply the difference, in decibels, between the sound level of the signal (the speech) and the sound level of the noise. Speech/reverberation ratios (S/R ratios) are defined in the same manner as S/N ratios, with the A-weighted sound level of the reverberant sound substituted for the A-weighted sound level of the noise. A good S/N ratio for speech intelligibility is a minimum of +15 dB greater than the background noise.

Reverberation time = RT60 of 0.4-0.6 second. Reverberation times are defined as the time in seconds required for the reverberant sound to decay 60 dB.

Meeting these criteria will ensure acoustical properties that enhance communication within the classroom for the vast majority of students, including those with some hearing impairment.

Building Systems Design. Integrated systems reduce overall noise. As advances in design move our buildings toward greater environmental sustainability, building systems will, necessarily, become more and more integrated. Mechanical systems will "read" lighting systems to better control heat and cooling loads; natural daylighting systems will be integrated with artificial lighting; and lighting systems will be integrated with security systems—which, in turn, will comprise part of the overall "intelligent building" system. This integration will continue until each of our buildings—including our schools— is a single intelligent system supporting the needs and desires of its users. Much of this technology is available and already in use today, so the time is not far off when totally integrated, intelligent, environmental/sustainable buildings become the norm.

A Glimpse of the Future

What will the elementary school classroom of the future look like? Chances are it won't look radically different from the classroom of today, but looks can be deceiving. Technology will likely drive much of the furniture and equipment selection, and instruction will increasingly depend on global communications using the Internet. Sound-wise, the room will suit its purpose—with the furniture and finishes enhancing the room's acoustical properties. Acoustical treatments will include a mixture of reflective and absorptive surfaces that can be adjusted, or "tuned," to the needs of particular users and particular activities.

Acoustical ceilings will continue to be used, though their noise-reduction coefficients will be enhanced. As in today's classrooms, floor coverings will mix hard surfaces, such as tile, with soft, acoustically absorbent materials (including not only carpet but possibly other materials, such as cork-based products). The comfort systems—heating, cooling, and ventilation—will be acoustically transparent, as will the lighting systems.

The flexibility required in typical classrooms confounds most attempts to design an acoustically perfect classroom. Engineers—including acoustical consultants—rely on some constant to which they can apply variables in order to make and test assumptions about how a space will work in actual use. In elementary school classrooms, the only constants are the physical dimensions of the space. The length and width of the room will not change (except where movable partitions are used), and the ceiling height is also constant. But classroom acoustical design that uses only fixed sound reflectors will be ineffective if the sound source is relocated—for example, if the room has been designed for a teaching station at an end wall but the teacher's desk is moved to a side wall. If, however, the designer strategically places adjustable sound reflectors/absorbers on the walls—treatments that can be easily manipulated by the users—the room can be acoustically tuned to changing configurations. The ceiling can be designed with a mixture of soft and hard surfaces by alternating high-NRC (noise reduction coefficient) tiles with hard, gypsum-type panels located so as to distribute the sound effectively to the entire room without excessive reverberation times. This concept is now being utilized in corporate conference room ceilings to help contain the sounds around a large conference table. The right mixture of hard and soft surfaces in the ceiling grid will reflect the sound of the teacher's voice to the opposite end while reducing the reverberation time to prevent reflected sound from muddling the primary source. The same principle can be used for the wall surfaces: adjustable reflectors can be placed on the center sections of the walls while the corners are treated with absorptive surfaces.

In typical elementary schools of the future—like those of today—classrooms will be aligned along exterior walls to take best advantage of natural ventilation and daylight. In such an arrangement, at least one wall has windows, and the designer must keep in mind that glass is a sound-reflective material. Generally, some sort of shading device—usually a roll-up shade or adjustable blinds, either vertical or horizontal—is employed to control the amount of daylight entering the room. The opportunities for acoustic control that these shading devices provide are too often overlooked: if fabric curtains or fabric-based blinds are used, the room will also have an adjustable acoustical control device, much as one would see in a theater or auditorium but on a smaller scale.

The furniture should also play a role in enhancing room acoustics, and doors and partitions should be thoughtfully placed and constructed so as to reduce sound transmission from one side of the corridor to the other. Increasing the mass of a wall not only helps control lower-frequency sounds, it also augments the wall's value as a fire retardant.

The long-term switchover to renewable energy sources will have a beneficial side-effect, acoustically. Solar, geothermal, and fuel-cell systems, because they are relatively "passive," will reduce noise and thereby enhance speech intelligibility.

Acoustics versus Indoor Air Quality

No discussion of school-building acoustics would be complete without mentioning the ongoing debates between proponents of improved classroom acoustics and advocates of improved indoor air quality (IAQ). The IAQ advocates would like to eliminate materials that can support the growth of molds, mildew, fungi, or other microorganisms as well as those that contribute volatile organic compounds (VOCs) to the indoor environment. Unfortunately, these are typically the same materials that the advocates of good classroom acoustics would like to see added to rooms.

Carpet, for example, has some acoustical benefits. It absorbs higher frequency noise and provides a buffer between the furniture and the floor, reducing the noise created when furniture is moved around. But carpet can be a source of various biological and chemical contaminants that negatively impact the air quality of classrooms. If not meticulously maintained, carpet has the potential to become host to various molds, dust mites, and other biological contaminants. There is also a history of problems with new carpet releasing VOCs (either from the carpet itself or from the adhesives used to install it). The Carpet & Rug Institute has led the way to vast improvements in the off-gassing issue and makes stringent recommendations for maintenance. (For more information, visit the Carpet & Rug Institute's website, at <www.carpet-rug.com/ideal_Learning_environment_study.cfm>.) If carpet is properly maintained it can provide the acoustical benefits mentioned above, but if poorly maintained it can pose serious health risks.

Sound attenuation treatments inside ductwork are also controversial. Sound attenuation is usually achieved through the use of glass-fiber duct lining. This insulation, however, provides an environment for the amplification of molds, mildew, and fungi, which contaminate the airstream. The exposed glass fibers can also break off and float into the breathing-air zone. Air distribution systems can be designed in such a way, however, to keep noise at an acceptable level without the use of duct lining—for instance, by proper sizing of ducts and terminals and by careful placement of sound attenuators throughout the system. In cases where some sort of duct lining is unavoidable, one of the alternatives to exposed glass-fiber duct liners should be used. (This, of course, does not come without a cost.)

The materials used in typical lay-in acoustical ceiling tile—starch and cellulose—can also provide a medium for the growth of molds, mildew, and fungi. Even when the tiles are made of glass fiber with an organic binder in the glass matrix, exposure to moisture or even excessive humidity can foster the growth of molds. Manufacturers do offer antimicrobial treatments, but the long-term effectiveness of this option remains untested. The solution here is to control moisture, which requires a properly designed, balanced, and maintained HVAC system. Once again, it's a systems approach that provides the best solution.

After all is said and done, some schools will also want to factor in the possibility of using amplification systems, which can be adjusted to meet each room's specific acoustical conditions.

Chapter 13

Security in the Elementary School of the Future

For a school to play its important social and community roles well, it must provide an environment in which both children and adults feel safe and protected. Public awareness of recent incidents involving serious and even fatal violence in schools has highlighted the issue of school safety as never before. Random acts of extreme violence by students are as difficult to comprehend as they are to prevent, and high-school students can pose a significant threat to themselves, their peers, and teachers and administrators, as well. Fortunately, security concerns in elementary schools are a bit easier to predict and plan for.

A secured school environment is not a prison: it must never project a message of danger, which is hardly conducive to teaching or learning. Schools must foster a welcoming and open environment and provide a place for the entire community to come together. How, then, should designers address issues of general safety and protect against both intruders and safety risks from within? Let's look at the three main kinds of threats to security and safety.

General Safety Issues

Many general safety issues, like clean air and water, will be addressed by various building codes. Because these codes often do not extend to the site as a whole, and because they tend to specify minimum requirements, safety can often be improved by careful planning and thoughtful design.

A safety-conscious site design should include a marked separation of school bus traffic from other vehicular traffic at the site. Designing the bus circulation pattern to allow for right-hand drop-offs and pick-ups will obviate the need for students to cross in front of traffic. All directional signage should be simple and clear. The bus loading area itself should provide adequate queuing space to avoid crowding and help keep the area orderly when children arrive at and leave school. Students dropped off or picked up by parents should use a separate area, so that private vehicles do not interfere with the bus traffic.

Weather protection is a good idea, as it will help to keep children from running long distances to and from buses during inclement weather. Parking areas should be located near entrances, but not in the path to any exterior play area. Building service areas with frequent truck deliveries should be well separated from students' play areas. And roadways around the building should allow full access for both fire and emergency vehicles, as well as for regular police pass-bys.

Today's environmental regulations often require new building sites to include retention basins for the control of storm water drainage. These, and any natural bodies of water, should be considered potential hazards, and access to them should be controlled by fencing.

Intruders

Protection against intrusion should address break-ins, larceny, vandalism, and potential violence, but also issues such as the unauthorized removal of children from the school. Good protection against these security threats begins with top-notch door hardware and an integrated intrusion alarm system.

All doors should be fitted with contacts that notify a central alarm system when the door is ajar. This type of system can be internal to the building or linked to a security company or the local police department. Windows at ground level and those accessible from rooftops should be fitted with glass-break contacts. If the window is operable, it should open a maximum of six or eight inches. Laminated glass or polycarbonate glazing materials will protect against breakage. Security screens can be installed, but fire departments usually take issue with them, as they may limit access in emergency situations.

Another security-enhancement option is video surveillance. Cameras are mounted at entrances and exits, in corridors, and concealed in certain strategic locations. They send images to closed-circuit television monitors in a central location. A time-lapse videotape is usually made so it can be reviewed in the event of any incident. Users of these systems generally find them useful as deterrents. To be effective in real time, however, the TV screens need to be monitored at all times when the building is in use. Trained security personnel can then either report an incident or attempt to thwart the illegal activity. To be most effective as deterrents, the cameras should be visible rather than hidden, suggesting to potential perpetrators that their activities may be recorded and their identities discovered. Unfortunately, this strategy leaves the cameras themselves vulnerable to damage and vandalism.

Landscaping around the building should be kept low to eliminate potential hiding places. And the building itself should avoid nooks and hidden corners where perpetrators can hide. While strict adherence to the Force Protection Standards required for the construction of government installations may be excessive, they offer sound ideas for security relative to site design and may be consulted by school construction planners.

Internal Security Controls

Constant adult supervision is inarguably the best method for maintaining security. But how can enough adults be distributed throughout the school building to maintain security effectively? Decreasing the overall enrollment can dramatically improve security and safety. Having fewer students makes it easier for adults to know, or at least recognize, everyone in the building. Strangers or intruders can be easily recognized and either approached or reported. Student bullies will be less likely to act out if they can be easily identified and deterred. Conversely, anonymity offers potential perpetrators a safe haven. It is much easier for those with bad intentions to remain anonymous in large schools.

Checklist

Here are a few other design ideas for increasing and maintaining security in a school building:

- Decentralize departments, faculty offices, and administrative offices to facilitate the deployment of adults throughout a building.

- Combine emergency communications stations, or "request for assistance" alarms, with video surveillance, to cut down on the rate of false alarms.

- Keep sight lines in corridors free from visual impediments. Plan the lengths of corridors so that a person standing at one end can easily recognize a person standing at the other. Build wide corridors to prevent overcrowding and the kind of incidental bumping in crowded hallways that can lead to altercations among students.

- Utilize only one entrance if the others must go unmonitored.

- Provide staff with reliable communications devices while monitoring outdoor and indoor activities.

- Make a staff of security-trained personnel available at all times while the building is occupied.

- Limit vehicular access to the site, with one way in, one way out, and an emergency access road with a gate.

- Establish "lock down" procedures that keep students contained and accounted for during emergency situations. Make sure that staff and students are drilled in these procedures. The goal should be to freeze conditions in the building until an emergency situation can be brought under control.

- Install a microchip-based identification system, like those that use swipe cards, to control access to the building, especially for adults. These devices can also record personal identification information, and help deter kidnapping or other unauthorized removals of children from the school.

Chapter 14

Indoor Air Quality— Problems and Solutions

Elementary schools of the future will be housed in buildings both new and old. Indoor air quality (IAQ) problems show no preference for old or new construction—new buildings have problems just as older buildings do. The fundamental issue in all IAQ problems is the pollutant source. In this chapter, we look at the various sources of indoor air contamination, then describe some basic principles for improving IAQ in future schools.

Volatile Organic Compounds

In new buildings, IAQ problems often involve either chemical off-gassing or inadequate ventilation. Finishing materials used in new construction go through a curing process during which some of the chemicals used in their manufacture are volatilized into the air, yielding what are referred to as VOCs, or volatile organic compounds. (Volatile in this case refers to the material's instability in its natural state—solid or liquid—and its tendency to change into a vaporous state at room temperature.) These chemical compounds, some man-made and some naturally occurring, evaporate at varying rates, after which they are present in the air. Some compounds, like alcohol or acetone, evaporate very rapidly; others, like the oily substances used to create residues in spray pesticides or smoothness in alkyd-based paints, evaporate so slowly that they are referred to as SVOCs, or semi-volatile organic compounds. We usually recognize VOCs as odors, but they don't always have a smell. VOCs are not necessarily dangerous; their toxicity depends on the compound itself and the level of someone's exposure to it. Chemical compounds like benzene (carcinogenic) or formaldehyde (reasonably anticipated to be carcinogenic) are hazardous to human health, but perfumes, air fresheners, and citrus fruit oils are also considered VOCs.

There are many potential product sources of these chemicals in new buildings. The most common are paints, adhesives, sealants and caulking, resilient flooring materials, carpet, and some furniture components. (It should be mentioned that some indoor air pollutants result from the activities that go on in school buildings every day. Among the VOCs that belong in this category are fumes and odors from consumable materials such as Magic Markers, cleaning fluids, and chemicals used in copying machines and printers.)

Careful and knowledgeable specification of finishing materials can reduce VOCs. Project specs should require sheet-type materials, such as carpeting, to be aired out prior to installation in the building. This process allows the majority of chemical residues to evaporate outside the new facility. The amount of off-gassing decreases very quickly in the first few days in most materials, but each material has its own requirements.

Another effective way to improve air quality is to air out the building itself. This involves setting the mechanical systems to maximum ventilation for a specified period of time prior to occupancy. (The heating system should never be used to "bake out" the building: this has a tendency to drive VOCs into other materials that can later release the chemicals after occupancy.)

This airing-out period can present a problem, however, since school projects usually adhere to very tight schedules utilizing each and every day leading up to the beginning of a school year. But early planning—and a schedule that treats the airing-out period as an essential step in the construction process—can help to prevent IAQ problems.

Other Gaseous Pollutants

Other gaseous pollutants may originate from site-related causes. Radon gas, a naturally occurring, colorless, odorless, radioactive element, is a common problem. Radon is easily mitigated with simple exhaust systems that use fans to pull the gas from the adjacent soil and vent it into the atmosphere above the occupied level. Soil gases may be leeched by leaking underground fuel tanks or previous site uses such as landfill or other disposal; such possibilities should be disclosed in the initial pre-selection site assessment work—and, as is mentioned elsewhere in this book, such land should usually be eliminated as a potential site for an elementary school. Additional site-related pollutants include vehicular exhaust fumes and odors from trash containers that enter air intake systems.

Comfort System–Related Problems

A school's heating, ventilating, and air conditioning (HVAC) systems—also known as indoor comfort systems—are designed to specific criteria for ventilation rates and heating and cooling loads. Problems with such systems generally arise from their use rather than from their design. When working as designed, the systems create well-balanced comfort conditions within an occupied space. An appropriate amount of fresh (outdoor) air is supplied to the space and balanced with a certain amount of air exhausted from the same space. The fresh air brought into the space is conditioned, or modified, to a certain temperature and, depending on the local climate, a certain humidity. The temperature and humidity can be modulated in various ways, but the air delivered to the space needs to be balanced with the air vented to avoid a buildup of carbon dioxide (CO_2). The fans that move the air, the air volume dampers in the ductwork, and all the grilles and diffusers are adjusted for proper air distribution. Temperature and humidity controls are calibrated and set to normal comfort ranges.

Ideally, after the systems are balanced, an independent contractor "commissions" the building systems. This involves activating all the systems in normal operating mode under normal operating conditions and verifying that all system components are in proper working condition. The systems are then fine-tuned and any substantial remedial work completed before the occupants move in. Even then, some additional remediation may be needed, as CO_2, humidity, and heat levels fluctuate with occupancy.

Ventilation air systems are presently designed for economy as well as efficiency. They recycle a certain amount of indoor air, mix this tempered air with fresh, outdoor air, and redistribute the blended air to the breathing zone. While this saves on heating and cooling, recycled air can become contaminated with pollutants or compromised by the presence of too much CO_2. (While CO_2 is not lethal, an overabundance can cause fatigue, lethargy, inattention, headache, irritability, and drowsiness) When this happens, the mechanical system becomes the distribution pathway for gaseous or particulate indoor air pollutants. Gaseous pollutants, such as the VOCs mentioned above, are chemical-based. Particulate pollutants can be biological, like molds, mildew, and fungi, or inorganic, like silica dust, asbestos, and fiberglass.

Operable Windows—The Downside

There is almost universal insistence on having operable windows in school buildings; but it is impossible for design engineers or HVAC system balancers to accurately predict their use. So the school's occupants themselves are a significant factor in operational problems. The conservative, practical approach plans on all windows and doors being shut. Problems then arise, of course, when windows or doors are opened, upsetting the balance of mechanically induced air ventilation. For example, open windows can reverse the airflow from a lavatory that has been designed with negative air pressure, causing odors to be forced back into a corridor. Open windows can also create localized ventilation loops that disrupt normal air distribution or cause a buildup of CO^2 in spaces occupied by groups of students.

Opening windows can bring about other indoor air quality problems, as well—which is somewhat ironic, since the object of opening windows is to bring fresh air indoors. When fertilizers and spray pesticides are applied outside open windows, these chemicals can easily make their way into a building. Open windows can also allow entrance of insects and other pests, as well as pollen and other plant allergens, all of which can impact the quality of the indoor environment. Dust and debris from adjacent areas can infiltrate, as can odors and fumes from outdoor activities. The problems are as variable as the use of the windows themselves, but, despite the greater mechanical efficiency of sealed buildings, most people still prefer the option of being able to open windows.

Typical ventilation systems for schools do not include filtration systems other than nuisance dust filters that affect only visible particulates. In the absence of such systems, the indoor air is only as clean as the outdoor air. While a variety of air purification systems have been developed, their efficacy and reliability remain largely untested. Systems such as ultraviolet sterilization, bipolar ionization, or photocatalytic cleansing of the ventilation air stream are available, but the up-front cost is usually prohibitive.

Biological Pollutants

While biological pollution is more common in older buildings, molds, mildew, and fungi can grow just as readily in a new building, given the right conditions. Mold spores are ubiquitous and at normal concentrations do not pose problems for most people. But when the right conditions are present, the spores can settle, the mold can multiply and release more spores, and, in just a matter of days, concentrations in the air can become significant enough to require remediation. The requirements for mold and fungus growth are darkness (or, more accurately, the absence of ultraviolet light), moderate temperature, high humidity or moisture, and a food source such as cellulose or some other organic material. These conditions are not uncommon inside wall cavities or in ceiling plenum spaces—hidden areas where mold growth may be difficult to locate until it is so extensive it becomes visible on the exposed surfaces, by which point the problem is very significant.

People's reactions to mold and fungus exposure vary. Some people may merely perceive a nuisance odor, while others react with life-threatening illness; the intensity of reactions and symptoms are unpredictable. Susceptibility depends on age, health, genetic predisposition, exposure levels, and on the type of mold or fungus itself. Young children are, as a group, more vulnerable to exposure than adults, making this a critical issue for elementary schools.

Certain types of molds and fungi are particularly toxic and require immediate attention if identified (for detailed information, see New York City Department of Health, 2000). Experts in the field of industrial hygiene should be consulted if a mold or fungus problem is suspected. They can identify the species, assess the scope of the contamination and risk, and make recommendations for a course of action. It is important to note that killing the mold or fungus only stops its amplification. Dead spores contain the same toxins as the viable spores. And dead spores are easily aerosolized if disturbed, entering the breathing zone and even the building's ventilation system. Remediation therefore often requires extensive site cleanup, with area containment similar to an asbestos remediation project.

The single most significant factor in the growth of biological pollutants is moisture, which can derive from a number of sources. In summer, warm air can condense on cool surfaces, such as pipes and air conditioning ducts, non-thermal windows and doors, or the uninsulated underside of roof decks in the cool of early morning hours. Moisture can come from leaking plumbing or roofs, from liquid spills, or from rain infiltrating through windows or walls. Significant moisture is tracked into a building on rainy days by people entering the space. Routine cleaning procedures typically use water. In other words, the sources of moisture are many, common, and everyday.

The best way to control biological pollutants is to control moisture. Repair leaks immediately and clean up spills as they happen. Use dry-cleaning techniques where possible, and force-dry areas where water is used. Quickly mop up rainwater tracked into the building. Do not let moisture sit anywhere for more than a few hours. If the local climate dictates, install humidity controls to keep the interior relative humidity to 45 percent or less, and insulate pipes and ducts against condensation. If the building is kept dry, molds, mildew, and fungi will not propagate.

Inorganic Particulate Pollutants

Particulate pollutants also derive from building materials. Older buildings—those built up until the early 1970s—probably contain asbestos insulation. Most school districts have cleaned up their buildings in accordance with the federal Asbestos Hazard Emergency Response Act (AHERA) of 1986. Remaining asbestos-containing materials should be catalogued and strictly managed so that they pose no threat to air quality. While asbestos is no longer used in school construction, today's fiberglass, mineral wool, fiber-type thermal and acoustic insulation, and some spray-on fireproofing materials used on structural steel can still contribute to airborne dust problems if not properly specified and installed.

IAQ in the Future Elementary School

So far, we've mostly focused on IAQ problems. So how do we go about ensuring good IAQ in the elementary school of the future? For new buildings the solution is straightforward. Provide 100-percent fresh air, tempered to comfortable temperature and humidity, at a rate that suits the occupants and their activities, rather than designing to minimum codes or guidelines. Never recycle exhaust air into the breathing zone. Displacement air ventilation systems that provide this volume of fresh air have proved successful—one example is the system used in the Boscawen School in Boscawen, New Hampshire, which was designed by the H. L. Turner Group and which was given an Environmental Merit Award by the U.S. Environmental Protection Agency in 1996 (Sustainable Buildings Industry Council, 2001).

If the outdoor air is fouled by smog, dust, or other industrial pollution, the building should include air-cleaning filtration within the ventilation system and the number and control of operable windows should be limited. The ventilation system should, through the use of sensors and controllers, compensate for temporary pressure imbalances caused by operable windows.

For renovated buildings, the systems mentioned above must be adapted to the existing space, and the cost/benefit ratio must be diligently analyzed. Adapting systems to fit existing building parameters is, by its nature, custom work that will increase the design and construction costs of a project. Perhaps the physical constraints of the building or the cost of adapting the systems will be such that the building is no longer even appropriate for school use. Educational planners need to be aware of indoor air quality issues, and IAQ must be considered in the early planning stages of a project to help make this very difficult programmatic decision.

A few final cautions are necessary. The first concerns facility maintenance. Keeping a building clean and dry is the formula for keeping it healthy. But the goal of a clean and dry building must be attained with the thoughtful and judicious use of environmentally sensitive cleaning methods and products. Schools are becoming increasingly specialized, high-performance technical buildings. As such they require a certain level of expertise to maintain them, much the way a high-performance vehicle requires specialized maintenance. These solutions do not come without added cost, but that cost must be balanced against the need for healthy indoor air—a requirement for good health and improved learning.

Second, educators need to be aware that there are many factors—improper lighting, excessive noise or vibration, overcrowding, poor ergonomics—that can produce symptoms similar to those associated with poor indoor air quality. In addition to ensuring the quality of the indoor air, these other stressors must be controlled for overall indoor environmental comfort.

Chapter 15

A Sustainable Approach to Elementary School Design

Architecture worldwide changed forever when the Organization of Petroleum Exporting Countries (OPEC) embargoed the United States and other western countries in 1973, causing widespread shortages in fossil fuels. Energy efficiency suddenly became paramount in design, and building codes and standards were revised to reflect the need to conserve energy and reduce reliance on oil. This new energy consciousness heightened interest in developing technologies such as solar and wind power. Unfortunately, when the embargo was lifted and OPEC's oil pipelines once again flowed freely westward, these technologies were marginalized, and never became part of mainstream commercial design. The relatively high up-front cost for these systems and a lack of demonstrable performance reliability proved to be the Achilles' heel of this emerging industry. It faltered and became a special-interest sector relegated to the back-page classifieds of industry periodicals.

The energy crisis of the early 1970s did, however, engender a persistent interest in environmental issues on both an academic and popular level. Today, as a generation of environmentally aware people assumes leadership positions in the professions, the idea of utilizing renewable resources and conserving nonrenewable ones is at last becoming mainstream. We find ourselves at the cutting edge of a 30-year-old idea: sustainable, or "green," design—design, that is, that treads lightly on the environment and works creatively with renewable resources.

Green Design

With this new (or restored) environmental awareness, architects are turning with great fervor to what are called holistic building techniques. And because there is general popular agreement that the environment matters, depletable resources are being conserved and renewable resources utilized. Schools are now designed with specific functional areas for recycling programs. Taking recycling one step further, thoughtful consideration of what a building might become after its initial function passes (adaptive reuse) is now part of the initial design process, and some components are designed to be recycled rather than demolished when a building is dismantled. Even building materials are designed and manufactured to be recycled into the same or different products. Carpet used to be torn out, hauled off to a landfill, and replaced. Today, recyclable carpets can be leased: the worn material is removed for recycling whenever new carpet is required. Though not always practiced, conservation of resources has become a mainstream idea.

In fact, capturing nature-provided energy resources is now standard technology for any who want to include such measures in a project. Geothermal heating and cooling—tapping into the constant ground temperature for climate control—is used increasingly in schools. Passive solar collection for hot-water heating is common. Production of electrical power through the use of photovoltaic collection devices (solar energy cells) is becoming a mature industry. Environmentally friendly technologies such as fuel cell electrical generation are gaining favor as their initial costs stabilize. Collect-

Julie A. Kim, AIA, contributed to this chapter.

ing rainwater for plumbing systems is coming to be considered conventional design, as is collection of wastewater for "gray water" irrigation systems. The use of highly reflective materials and colors to avoid heat buildup on large surfaces such as paved parking areas and large, flat roofs is an easy choice. And even more adventurous roofing strategies—like the grass-planted roofs for the Chicago public school discussed in Chapter 3—are finding proponents among public school designers. These are just a few of the green ideas being included in present-day designs.

A life-cycle cost analysis of various building materials and systems should be part of any design decision-making process and is often mandated by regulatory agencies. These analyses consider not only what it costs to purchase, install, maintain, and eventually replace a material or system but also the costs of the energy required to collect, process, and transport the raw materials used in the manufacture, packaging, and delivery of the system. Along with the construction, installation, and maintenance costs, replacement and ultimate disposition costs of the materials through landfills or recycling now informs the selection of building components.

Likewise, sustainable design requirements are being met by manufacturers competing for "green" budget dollars. In fact, companies with generous R&D budgets are often leading the charge with new products. A good example—already referred to—is the carpet industry. With millions of tons of used carpeting filling up landfills, the carpet industry recognized a problem and moved forward to develop ideas in marketing and manufacturing technologies to reclaim these potential raw-material resources.

Sustainable products are hardly new to the marketplace. Some of the most sustainable materials are those that have been used in schools for the last hundred years, including exterior brick, masonry interior walls, ceramic tile, and terrazzo floors. In older school buildings these materials have long since paid for themselves in savings on maintenance expenses. But the quantity, variety, and availability of sustainable materials is greater now than ever before. In the long run, the use of such materials can be kind to both the environment and the operations budget. While it is the purview of the architect to make the best decisions for the specifics of the individual school program and budget, it is incumbent on him or her to make sure that project decision-makers are informed about life-cycle costs and are not bound by a first-cost-only mindset. A byproduct of the typical public-funding process, which establishes separate budgets for building a school and for maintaining and operating it, such thinking stands in the way of either a truly green or truly economically sound project.

The Future Meets the Present

As sustainable design techniques become fundamentals of design philosophy, a new building prototype is emerging. While the building may not look so different from the elementary school of today, it will operate very differently. Comfort systems will be much more user-controllable than they generally are today. As reliance on fossil fuels—and, hence, operating costs—decline, the strict controls now placed on building heating and cooling can become more lenient. If an individual room is too cool in the early morning hours, the users can adjust the heat to temporarily compensate. If it is overheating in the afternoon, the cooling can be increased. The central building intelligence system will register these adjustments and incorporate them into the building's day-to-day operating routines. If a classroom develops an over-abundance of fumes or odors, sensors will detect the imbalance and purge fans will engage to ventilate the room to proper fresh-air levels.

Advances in lighting technology are already providing balanced illumination and color temperature approximating natural daylight. Other lighting system-related architectural strategies and electronic features—all available now—will come into greater use in tomorrow's elementary schools. Light shelves (horizontal devices with a reflective surface) will redirect daylight into building interiors, decreasing the need for artificial light and reducing electric-power consumption. The lighting control system will read the level of daylight entering an interior and correct the balance of natural and artificial illumination for the time of day and the solar orientation of the room. Lighting control systems will communicate with the building management system and adjust the heating, ventilating, and air conditioning (HVAC) systems to economize on heating or cooling, depending on lighting conditions.

It's a point well worth making that green design has two equally important aspects: it's good for the environment and it's good for the human occupants of a building. That double function can be clearly seen, for example, in the push to maximize natural daylighting of interior spaces. Not only does natural daylighting improve the interior environment for those who study and work there, but it also reduces electricity bills. That, in turn, lessens dependence on the fossil fuels often used to generate electricity and therefore reduces a building's contribution to air pollution in general.

The State of Connecticut recently mandated that school districts consider maximizing natural light in new school buildings as well as those undergoing alteration or renovation. Why? because natural daylight is a great mood enhancer, which can lead to greater attentiveness, improved attendance, and higher achievement. (Some strategies for maximizing natural daylight, even in interior spaces far from windows, are discussed in Chapter 3, "The Elementary School of Today: Four Exemplary Projects," in the section on the Southwest School in Torrington, Connecticut.)

In the elementary school of the future, communications systems will be merged. The public address system will no longer be separate from the telephone/intercom system. Communications devices will be part of an integrated VDV (voice, data, video) network, which itself will be part of a larger intelligent building system that incorporates security, life safety, and building management systems, as well. Imagine the intimacy of a school in which the principal makes routine announcements to all students via video conferencing to each classroom, rather than through wall-mounted speakers that distort sound. Many of these technologies are available today, although the complexity of programming and operating them will require that the staff of the school of the future include trained network systems managers.

Classroom acoustical problems will be resolved through the strategic use of materials that reflect, diffuse, or absorb sound. (This topic is addressed in detail in Chapter 12, "Improving School Acoustics—A Systems Approach.") Indoor air quality will no longer be an issue, as the building will be infused with conditioned fresh air. Displacement ventilation systems might well replace the ducted central air systems, fed from rooftop air handlers, that are currently used. As filtration technology advances, the indoor air will be as clean as—and quite possibly cleaner than—the outdoor air. (For more on this topic, see Chapter 14, "Indoor Air Quality: Problems and Solutions.")

A Sustainable Approach to Siting/Site Design

The individual school's specific requirements and the character of the surrounding environment must drive the site selection process. Urban schools usually have a vertical orientation because of the shortage of suitable real estate in cities. Suburban schools face transportation-related site issues: Where can buses queue? Where can parents, driving their own cars, drop off their kids in the morning and wait to pick them up in the afternoon? Regional schools generally require large athletic fields and facilities. All schools have to deal with deliveries and services.

While site selection is project-specific, there are some sustainable criteria that ought to be considered in any elementary school site selection process. For example, sites where mass transportation is both available and likely to be used will reduce the number of trips in private motor vehicles—and thus pollution. Proximity to population centers encourages the use of nonpolluting modes of transportation such as bicycles and walking. Schools should not be located near major industrial facilities, near trucking routes or other heavily traveled highways, or on or near sites that are toxically contaminated or that, because of past use, may present some environmental health hazard. While this last point seems obvious enough, schools have in fact been built on top of landfills, and there is currently a push, through the use of tax incentives, for the development of so-called brownfield sites (reclaimed former industrial or manufacturing sites). While brownfield sites can be successfully cleaned up and may be judged environmentally sound, brownfields might best be developed by private industry and not used for purposes that involve young children—purposes that would make it difficult to justify even a miniscule risk of exposure to toxic contaminants. (Siting issues are covered in detail in Chapter 11, "Site Design and Landscape Architecture for the Future Elementary School.")

Other sustainable design ideas include capitalizing on what might otherwise be considered site problems. In a suburban setting, wetlands and animal habitat issues frequently become problematic. In a sustainably designed school, these will become onsite educational assets—tools for teaching about ecology and conservation. Geological problems with bedrock or poorly draining soils can lead to a sanitary waste disposal problem. A sustainable approach would involve onsite processing, whether by a packaged sewage disposal processing plant or some other alternative processing technique. This, too, might serve as an educational asset, acquainting students with recycling and biomechanical processes.

Future Use of the School Building Itself

Sustainable design includes thinking about the future, both near and far. Near-future concerns address the building construction costs and schedule, and the operating costs in terms of both dollars and the environment. Far-future considerations include the possibility that the building may someday become obsolete as a school because of pedagogical changes, demographic shifts, or other reasons. Could it someday be utilized for municipal offices, housing, business, manufacturing or warehousing—without major reconstruction and needless waste of resources? If these changes can be planned for in the present, the life of a building can be extended by decades.

If major reconstruction would be required to convert the building to some other function, could the materials removed from the building be reused or recycled? All the materials that go into a building need to be considered for their recycling potential. Metals, such as steel, cast iron, aluminum, and copper, are easily recycled. Many plastics can be recycled to provide raw materials for other products. Non-pressure-treated wood products can be recycled into other wood or cellulose-based products. Some single-ply-membrane roofing products can be reclaimed. Even if the building itself cannot exist forever, its components may exist as sustainable resources for other buildings or as other products for decades to come.

Chapter 16

School Construction in the Future

by John D. Jenney, Richard S. Oja, AIA, and Edward Weber, PE

Building Infrastructure

In 1998, the Department of Energy initiated a "Building for the 21st Century" initiative to promote the "whole building" approach to the design of commercial buildings. This approach is intended to promote collaboration between the architectural and engineering disciplines in developing building designs that are not only functional but also energy efficient, healthy, flexible, and sustainable. As designers, contractors, and manufacturers get on board with this approach, the benefits will filter out of the commercial building industry into the arena of public-sector construction, exerting a profound influence on the way schools are designed.

Energy Efficiency. A number of new building-systems technologies—including passive solar radiation, solar energy, fuel cells, and thermal storage, among others—will find their way into the mainstream. As the production and use of these systems increase, the associated construction and installation costs will decrease, and the initial cost of these systems will become more competitive with current energy systems. Ultimately, the use of these new technologies will result in a win-win situation for school districts and everyone else. Reduced energy consumption will mean lower utility bills. And reductions in the output of hydrocarbons (produced by combustion heating systems) will have a positive impact on the environment generally.

Air Quality. Some existing schools, using an inadequate supply of outside air for ventilation and having little or no means of controlling humidity, become "sick" from the dust, CO_2 buildup, and mold growth associated with these flawed building systems. Building materials containing formaldehyde, solvents, asbestos, and lead exist in many schools. In many cases, their negative effects are compounded by inadequate outside air and filtration.

To address air quality in schools, designers will need to provide greater volumes of fresh, outside air. With the increase in air, however, come compromises that must be addressed architecturally. Mechanical spaces must be sized to accommodate larger air-handling equipment. Exposed ductwork, once unheard of in building design, will become commonplace as size requirements necessitate the installation of ducts below ceilings. Even the days of thru-wall unit ventilators may be numbered, as filtration and humidification/dehumidification requirements lead to greater use of ducted, central-station air-handling systems.

Another aspect of air quality that has increasingly become a matter of concern is mold growth. Once dismissed as an unavoidable byproduct of leaky roofs, this microbiological contaminate has been linked to "sick" buildings around the country. To prevent new schools from falling victim to this syndrome, designers will have to specify more sophisticated dehumidification and filtration devices in schools' heating, ventilating, and air-conditioning (HVAC) systems. In addition, designers need to rethink building-skin construction to reduce the potential for water infiltration. (For a detailed discussion of indoor air quality issues, see Chapter 14.)

Building Management Systems. As systems that control the indoor environment grow more sophisticated, so too must the equipment that controls them. The benefits of building management systems (BMSs) that allow integrated control of ventilation, heating, cooling, and lighting systems are becoming more evident. Such systems optimize performance, comfort, and energy efficiency. Their components include sensors and building-system time schedules that turn lights and HVAC systems on and off on based on an area's usage.

Sophisticated BMSs can also monitor the health of the systems they control. Filters, valves, fans, and dampers can all be monitored by the BMS, giving maintenance personnel early warning of trouble and enabling them to fix a problem before it becomes a failure. Ultimately, this will reduce system downtime and repair costs.

Security. Security systems are increasingly being treated as key, integral components of a school building's overall design. In addition to monitoring doors to protect unauthorized entry from the outside, cameras, security guards, and emergency response stations will be utilized by schools to deter theft, vandalism, and other crimes.

Building Materials

School Buildings' Life Expectancy. "They don't build 'em like they use to" applies to schools, too. Schools built in the early 20th century were usually built with a life expectancy of roughly 75 years. For the past 50 years, though, new schools were built to last only 25 to 35 years, on average. This change can be attributed to many factors, including budget constraints and material availability. Recent advances in building materials, however, will permit us to reverse this trend.

First Costs versus Life-Cycle Costs. Building materials have undergone an evolution. Traditional materials such as wood, stone, brick, steel, and plaster have been supplemented by—or in some cases replaced by—metal framing, concrete masonry units (CMUs), precast concrete, metal panels, and gypsum wallboard. And the list of materials from which a designer may choose is getting longer. When considering building material alternatives, designers must figure in life-cycle costs: For example, will the upfront savings realized by using gypsum wallboard instead of CMUs offset the long-term maintenance costs associated with the less durable material? Similar questions apply no matter which building component—roof, skin, interior—is being designed.

Prefabrication. Pre-engineered building products such as precast concrete, prefabricated steel structures, and curtain-wall assemblies have dramatically changed the construction industry. These materials have three distinct advantages over traditional materials: they save time, they reduce cost, and (in many cases) they ensure quality. It seems that many projects these days are "fast track" in nature. This approach, however, seldom recognizes the fluctuations of weather and labor availability. To remedy this, prefabricated building components will become standard features in tomorrow's buildings. Precast concrete panels, for example, not only offer the durability of concrete, but the material can usually be installed in a much broader range of weather conditions. On a greater scale, school construction will realize the gains made in the residential construction industry because of large-scale "panelized" construction. Wall, floor, and roof assemblies will be factory-fabricated under tight quality control, then be installed quickly and without need for specialized technicians, reducing the demand for the traditional trades—carpentry, masonry, etc.—where skilled workers are already in short supply. Designers benefit from prefabricated components because the quality of the work can be guaranteed and because the shops producing these products can construct virtually any assembly that a designer can put down on paper. Installers benefit because prefabricated components reduce construction time and make weather and labor less critical factors. Owners benefit because of decreased construction time, lower cost, and standardized quality.

Reduced Need for Skilled Labor. As "panelized" construction reduces the need for skilled labor, so, too, do other building materials. Advances in plastics will transform the way that buildings are plumbed. PEX (cross-linked polyethylene) pipe, for example, will no longer be used just in residential construction. Because of its durability, ease of installation, and low cost, this material (or other, similar plastic piping) will replace iron and copper pipe in domestic water piping, hot water heating, and fire protection systems. The comparative ease of installation will reduce the industry's reliance on highly skilled pipe and sprinkler fitters.

Maintenance

Building Management Systems. A BMS is only as good as the people who operate it. If a system alarm indicates that a filter is failing, maintenance personnel should be able to respond quickly and expertly. If a pressure sensor or valve actuator is malfunctioning, the BMS system will know it, but it's the maintenance department that is ultimately responsible for making repairs. Municipalities must understand that although technology will improve the operation and performance of building systems, maintenance departments must be able to keep up with technological changes. That means receiving sufficient funding to adequately train personnel and to keep manpower levels high enough to operate building systems effectively.

Outsourcing. One approach to providing the trained personnel necessary for operating sophisticated building systems is outsourcing. Although this approach to control costs has seen a downturn in recent years, many municipalities may find that keeping qualified maintenance personnel in-house may be cost-prohibitive. In many cases, school districts may decide to link all their schools' BMSs to one central location, from which vantage an "outsourced "engineering staff will be able to monitor and respond to building system problems, either via in-house maintenance staff or local contractors.

Construction Delivery Methods

Traditionally, school construction has been performed according to a design-bid-build sequence in which:

- The building design is completed by the architect.
- The project is advertised and an invitation to bid on the project is distributed.
- General contractors (GCs) respond by obtaining the bid packages and procuring bid prices from subcontractors.
- On the advertised date, the bids are opened publicly and read aloud to all attending the bid opening.

In this model, the low bidder is—after some reference-checking—generally awarded the contract, and construction begins. During construction, the architect monitors the project to ensure that the contractor is executing the work in accordance with the construction documents and the design intent.

Architects, generally speaking, prefer to design buildings. Trying to shepherd the low-bid contractor through a project successfully is a task that few architects enjoy, and, at least in the public domain, monitoring construction has been considered the "grunt work" of the profession. The goals of the owner (i.e., the school district), the GC, and the architects are not always aligned. The owner wants to avoid budget and schedule overruns; the GC wants to make a profit and keep his workforce employed; and the architect wants proper execution of the design intent.

These differing goals created an opening for a new kind of entity, the construction manager (CM). Neither a general contractor nor a design firm (although construction managers have emerged from both), the CM takes control of the "dirty work"—the construction phase—managing the construction process as the owner's representative. In the past, owners would employ a clerk of the works or a resident engineer, depending on the size and complexity of the project, but these positions were basically construction monitors, reporting to owner or architect, and lacked any specific contractual powers. The CM, on the other hand, does hold the contractual enforcement powers and manages the project on that basis.

Today, CM contracts come in two forms:

- *CM as constructor*, in which the CM contracts directly with all the subcontractors required on the project, or
- *CM as adviser*, in which the powers of enforcement are given to the CM but the subcontracts are held by the owner, giving the owner more financial control but also the additional burden of managing the financial minutiae of a construction project.

Architects are not lost in this process: they are still involved as advisers on the interpretation of the contract documents and continue to be responsible for their design and documents.

Subcontractors that perform well on a project are likely to be selected by the CM for future projects, so they have more motivation to be efficient than they do under the general contractor model, where everybody is a low bidder and future work depends only on making a low bid.

Today and into the future, we increasingly see the CM coming on board well before the construction phase. Owners are hiring CMs during the design phase to advise on cost control during design, constructability, phasing (particularly on occupied renovation projects), and overall schedule. The CM's role is often being expanded into what is called *program management*. The program manager oversees the entire process—project initiation, hiring the architect, design, and construction.

The CM process has proved successful, but it is worth noting that the addition of another management layer does mean an additional outlay of fees. Typically, the CM's fee is based on a percentage of the construction cost fee as well as reimbursables. The percentage range will depend, of course, on the scale and scope of the project: the larger the project, the lower the percentage.

Chapter 17

Exceptional Kids Need More Feet: Designing Barrier-Free Schools for Special Education Students

At Trumbull High School in the Bridgeport suburb of Trumbull, Connecticut, the Planning and Placement Team applauded junior Shane Spencer's involvement with the audiovisual club and developed an Individual Educational Plan (IEP) for him that called for AV club participation before and after school. Shane's father and mother, who were deeply involved with development of the plan, pointed out that, although the concept was fine, it wouldn't work because Shane, a student with multiple disabilities who is confined to a wheelchair, could not open the school's front door.

After lengthy discussion with the Trumbull Board of Education, it was determined that an electronic door opener costing $2,400 would solve the problem. An agreement, in keeping with the IEP, was reached in which the Board of Ed would install the opener, paying for the device and associated construction costs out of emergency/contingency facility funding.

During the same period, the Trumbull district determined that it needed an alternate education facility for approximately 50 high school students, some identified as special education students and many with emotional and related behavior problems. The district decided that this facility should be configured into existing middle school space. The facility was designed with IEP requirements in mind, and a substantial effort was made to accommodate different students' varying needs. Costs associated with this renovation added up to approximately $200,000.

Another Connecticut high school, this one in the Hartford suburb of Plainville, recently faced an uncomfortable dilemma. In response to a state ruling declaring that playing-field press boxes must be fully accessible, school officials shut down their football field's press box—part of a structure built long before disabled-access legislation was ever introduced—as they searched for an affordable and workable solution. As they investigated the possibility of installing a lift—having already decided that constructing a wheelchair ramp would be infeasible or prohibitively expensive—the old press box went unused.

Educational Entitlements and School Architecture

School districts across the country are facing extraordinary demands on their facilities. The reasons for the seemingly inexorable increases in space needs are many—including, for example, rocketing enrollments, the expansion of community recreational programs, and curriculum development that focuses on providing space for collaboration, hands-on activities, and a problem-solving approach to learning. But one of the prime movers pushing up space requirements is the expansion of educational entitlements due children with disabilities resulting from the Individuals with Disabilities Education Act (IDEA) of 1990. That federal law, combined with the Americans with Disabilities Act (ADA) of 1990 and with state laws and local mandates, has created a situation in which schools' legal and moral obligations to attend to the needs of special education students sometimes conflict with districts' facility and financial resources. Much of the space and money crunch happens at the high school level, but the problems certainly aren't limited to high schools. IDEA extended protections and entitlements to children younger than five years of age, which means that many school districts are wrestling with questions about how to provide barrier-free access to educational opportunity from the earliest preschool years through 12th grade.

School officials are hardly unaware of these developments—or of the space and financial quandaries they so often raise. Yet, to our knowledge, there has been no comprehensive study of the impact that disabilities/special education legislation and case law has had on school districts nationally. Although there have been numerous attempts to study the problem and many special hearings on the topic before national, state, and local legislative bodies, supportive data falls short of being comprehensive. It is just too difficult to uncover all the expenditures or to discern their rationales—or, in fact, to determine with any precision the relationships between particular expenditures and the special education needs that instigated them. For instance, what indicator, other than a transcript of the Board of Ed discussion itself, could possibly lead to uncovering the Trumbull electronic door-opener expenditure? The actual expense was buried in an emergency facility fund. There is a paucity of information about the strategies that districts pursue to make sure that the architectural design of new and renovated schools meets special education and related space needs. If such information were systematically compiled, it might help districts contain costs related to special education, now and in the long run.

In the absence of a national or systematic study, we can offer only anecdotal evidence of the kinds of challenges school districts are facing. But that evidence is, we believe, telling, and it has led us to speculate on the architectural ramifications of special education entitlements. What follows is a discussion of these implications, with an eye toward helping school officials prepare to work with architects to ensure that special education needs are met. Of course, the financial pinch that school districts feel is partly created by the fact that state reimbursements have not caught up with the increased square-footage demands arising from special education entitlements and other factors. Legislative action on this score is, unfortunately, likely to be long in coming. In the meantime, school officials need concrete advice on how to best serve all of a districts' students while keeping special education-related costs as low as possible. As we'll indicate, this is a very tall order indeed.

Specific Space Implications

In the decade since ADA and IDEA were signed into law, Americans (architects included) have learned quite a lot about how to accommodate people with physical disabilities and to ensure their easy access to all sorts of facilities. We have a fair amount of experience and now deal reasonably well with access issues involving elevators, entranceways, (including the provision of ramps and interior automatic doors), lavatories, and so on. We still have a long way to go, however.

As a society, we haven't yet come to grips with some of the subtler aspects of disabilities legislation, which aims at ensuring that disabled people participate equally in all the opportunities that we provide to the able-bodied. In schools, this means making sure that, to the greatest degree possible, physically disabled students are able to enjoy access to all parts of the curriculum as well as all extracurricular activities. For instance, we can no longer relegate student clubs or groups, like the yearbook editorial team, to constricted, inaccessible, out-of-the-way offices or storage rooms. If a wheelchair-bound student wants to serve as a manager of the football or field hockey team, architecture and landscaping must serve his or her wishes: locker rooms must be fully accessible, as must playing fields and, as we saw above, auxiliary facilities such as press boxes.

So far, this seems simple enough in concept, and the space (and cost) implications might seem relatively clear. In actuality, they can be exceedingly complex. To take just a few examples: When designing new school gymnasiums or rehabbing old ones, architects must take pains to ensure that bleachers are accessible, which might involve the addition of ramps, the implementation of new handhold standards, and the like. Such measures aren't only expensive; they also have an impact on space. (In a renovated gym, the number of seats might be reduced by as much as 20 percent to permit these kinds of changes.) Making a school's pool accessible might involve the installation of an electric lift to lower physically disabled students into the water. Here again, there isn't just a cost impact (the expense of the equipment) but a space impact as well. The poolside areas must be larger or differently configured in order to accommodate the apparatus.

The list of architectural interventions necessary to accommodate physically disabled students has grown quite long—and the impact on space and budget is burgeoning accordingly. In auditorium design, for example, it's no longer satisfactory to designate a certain seating area for wheelchairs; such spaces should be scattered around the house, so that wheelchair-bound students—like all others—have a choice of vantage. Lifts must be provided to enable disabled students to access the pit and the control room.

The design of band and choral group practice rooms must likewise be reconceived: the old tiered arrangement turns out to be impractical for disabled-access purposes in most school buildings, since wheelchair ramps capable of servicing all the tiers are expensive—and require that the room be enormous, since the angle at which such ramps can incline is very slight. (Flat-floored band rooms eliminate the access problem but create difficulties with sightlines and acoustics for which solutions must be found.)

Hallway design must factor in a host of variables relating to access: For instance, wheelchair-accessible water fountains typically protrude fairly far into corridors and may necessitate increasing corridor width. (And, for school buildings, such fountains and their mountings must be extra-strong, since athletically inclined students tend to use them as ad hoc pommel horses!) Corridors must incorporate buzzer-equipped "refuge" spaces to which wheelchair-bound students can retreat when having difficulties or in case of fire. To aid visually impaired students, all hallway signage must include Braille versions, and doors to off-limits rooms must have knurled knobs to warn against entering those areas. And lab design, too, must accommodate students with disabilities—including the provision of special-height counters for students using wheelchairs.

It's also important to point out that "barriers" don't just consist of the physical impediments—walls, stairs, doors—restricting disabled students' movement. A "barrier" can involve what is not there as much as what is. For example, not only do some assistive devices (e.g., wheelchairs) require space, but many electronic assistive devices require recharging stations; and space for these is not usually anticipated in a school's design. A barrier limiting a physically disabled child's equal access to educational opportunity is thereby being erected "by omission," one might say.

Planning and Placement Team Facilities

Most facility modifications are drawn from decisions taken by the federally mandated Planning and Placement Teams that exist in all public schools across the nation. These teams make decisions based on what they think is realistically possible. If, for example, a child is having a bad allergic reaction in a classroom, the PPT plan might call for installation of an air purifier and/or removal of a suspect rug. The use of whiteboards instead of blackboards has to some extent been driven by dust-related disability complications.

It's obvious that Planning and Placement teams need somewhere to meet. What may not be so obvious is that a well-functioning PPT meeting space has some relatively complex programmatic requirements.

First, the main PPT conference room must be fairly large. It isn't uncommon for a PPT meeting to include the following people: the student, his or her parents, as many as five teachers, a social worker, a guidance counselor, one or more representatives from the school district, one or two attorneys for the Board of Education, one or two attorneys or other advisers representing the student, a stenographer, and possibly a state appointed mediator. That list of participants, as long as it is, is not necessarily complete. This means we are talking about a conference room capable of comfortably accommodating upwards of 20 people. PPT negotiations resemble other legal procedures, in which, for example, parties may at certain points wish to retire from the negotiations in order to consider offers, discuss strategy, and so on. Therefore, it may be advisable for the PPT space to be configured as a suite that includes a main conference room and one or more auxiliary "caucus" rooms where the parties can sequester themselves, if necessary.

PPT spaces also need to be private and, to ensure that recording equipment works properly, insulated against outside noise. They need to be air conditioned as well, since many PPT meetings occur during the summer months, before the beginning of the school year. (A given hearing may last for several days, which makes the need to air condition PPT spaces even more urgent). These combinations of requirements of size, privacy, quiet, and air conditioning mean that it is often wise to make PPT meeting spaces dedicated meeting spaces. Needless to say, setting aside an area of a school building specifically for this purpose can have a significant impact on overall square footage.

"Special Education": Expanding the Definition

In some ways, "Special Education," traditionally understood as applying to students with physical disabilities and/or diagnosable learning disabilities, may be too narrow and limiting a term to designate contemporary school districts' efforts to ensure equal educational opportunity for all students. Perhaps we ought instead to speak of "alternate education," a term that would cover not only the legally mandated special education strategies that are designed to assist children with physical and/or learning disabilities but also those strategies that districts are pursuing to ensure that students with family, emotional, or psychological problems also receive the fullest, best educational experience possible. (Many of these students are considered "pre-special education.")

To help students in this latter group, and to reduce the chance that students with emotional problems will disrupt other students' learning process, many schools today are employing techniques to help students manage their anger, and even to mediate disputes that arise among students at large, with the aim of preventing disagreements from escalating into more serious problems. These strategies, too, have very real effects on space needs and on how space is allocated. For example, whether a school relies on trained student mediators or a salaried anger-management/mediation specialist, rooms must be set aside for this purpose.

As we make progress in learning how to deal with wall, stair, and door barriers, technology is giving us the ability to deal with barriers of a different nature. When students cannot, for some legitimate reason, leave their homes to come to school, schools have traditionally sent tutors to provide at-home instruction. In a technologically enhanced educational environment, however, schools will in all probability be required to telecommunicate lessons in full-motion audio/video format utilizing the Internet or an intranet system. Likewise, computer technology provides in-school solutions for students who have problems hearing, seeing, and/or writing. Students with these kinds of difficulties can be assisted by district-owned laptops with earphones, large-print capabilities, and/or voice-recognition software.

The goal, of course, is inclusiveness: to make sure, whenever and wherever possible, that special-needs students are not segregated but have the opportunity and ability to learn, eat, play, study, and travel to and from campus with so-called "regular" students. The infrastructure necessary to support the new technology includes room for sophisticated wiring and switching gear, repair/maintenance space, production areas, training stations, and simple charging and disbursement stations. And these specialized space needs translate into extraordinary expense.

"Soft" Costs and Inflationary Factors

To appreciate the full impact on design and construction costs of accommodating special-needs students in all areas of academic life, one must also figure in the nearly unavoidable increases in "soft" costs that such efforts entail. For example, school-facility planning costs are proportionally higher than in the past: as case law and state regulatory decisions continue to mount, architects and planners have come to anticipate that a significant amount of redrawing will usually be necessary following state review of plans.

For a variety of reasons ranging from construction industry labor and building-material shortages to the decreasing availability of suitable sites for building new schools (and concomitant increases in the need to perform extensive site remediation before construction begins), inflation rates in school construction are already higher than the average across-the-board rates calculated by the Consumer Price Index. (The full set of factors driving up school construction costs is laid out in Chapter 2, "Cost, Change, and School Construction.") Accommodating students with disabilities exacerbates this inflationary trend because of the rise in the number of code-mandated requirements that must be incorporated into facility design and followed during construction.

Moreover, incorporating features that enhance access for students with disabilities inevitably widens the gap between gross and net square feet. School officials are sometimes puzzled by this, since the gross-to-net ratio can grow even when stringent efforts are made to limit a school facility's size—for instance, by reducing classroom dimensions. But there's really no mystery: many of the disabled-access and related elements mentioned above—wider corridors, hallway refuge spaces, recharging stations, rooms for air-conditioning equipment, and so on—have the effect of increasing gross square footage disproportionately.

Agreement, Knowledge, Patience, and Understanding

In the face of these stepped-up demands on school facilities, what can a school administration do to stem the tide of rising costs related to meeting exceptional student needs? The answer to the question is not abundantly clear, but some school districts have successfully implemented an administrative approach that emphasizes agreement among officials, sound knowledge and expert counsel, patience, and a willingness to understand parents' concerns. Below, we describe this approach—one that, in broad terms, could be adopted by any school district.

Educators are ethically and professionally charged with the task of doing what is right to meet students' needs and help them learn. On this basis, one might suggest that an administrator will always be on solid ground if he or she advocates paying the bill—no matter how high—for any apparently valid special needs request.

The problem is that some of the requests come with enormous price tags. For instance, supporting a residential placement for an emotionally disturbed student might require an annual expenditure on the part of the district of, say, $75,000. This, of course, would correspondingly reduce the amount of money available for other important educational projects. Knowing this, most administrators will try to hold off on making a large special education expenditure even where such an expenditure will be a step toward meeting an exceptional student's needs.

But, to contain special education-related expenditures successfully, the superintendent, the administrator in charge of special education, and the district's business manager must be in agreement about which requests to support, which to oppose, and where to draw the line. If a special education director takes an issue that has not been agreed upon to the Board of Education, a state mediator, and/or the Exceptional Children's Parents Organization, the director is likely to win the argument and the town to be forced to spend the money. The three administrators must therefore learn how to work together and to present a unified front.

In many cases, even when a school district administration presents a solid position opposing a parent's request, the parent will call for a hearing with the state's department of education or will go to court—and stands a good chance of winning a favorable decision. The Board of Education and district administration must therefore have the assistance of an adept and knowledgeable lawyer with experience in the special education field and knowledge of how the school administration, Board of Education members, state mediators, and the courts would be likely to react if pressed on a given issue. In preparing to deal with special education requests, districts have to be ready to "pay the price" by having a knowledgeable lawyer on staff, backed by a quality law firm on retainer.

Taking problems into the legal arena is not always prudent or wise, however. Understanding how a particular request accords with legal requirements and understanding something about the particular parent or parents making the request—being able to guess with some degree of certainty the kind of action they might take if the request is denied—are essential. For one thing, administrators must know when to "fold their cards" and grant a request. In many cases a partial solution to the problem may be acceptable enough that the district can delay having to lay out the comparatively huge amount of money that meeting the full request would require. And sometimes parents' concerns can be assuaged by less costly solutions—assigning a teacher's aid to provide tutoring, for example, or purchasing a laptop with special features designed to ease the student's learning difficulties. Getting all the parties to agree to accept an arbitrator's decision may be helpful in resolving some situations.

In all cases, human relations skills are absolutely necessary when dealing with parents who often feel that they are their children's' only advocates. The administration must exhibit patience and understanding. Many an advocate for exceptional children has been stonewalled by school administrators only to rebound and to win the argument with a resolution that is significantly more costly than the initial request. It always pays to bend over backwards to support special education students, their parents, and their advocates in booster groups and parent/teacher associations. Making a real effort to understand the challenges that students with disabilities face goes a long way toward bridging communication gaps.

The record is full of cases where what appeared to be a minority position turned out to have majority support. In the 1999/2000 school year, again in Trumbull, Connecticut, the district administration and eventually the Board of Education agreed to fight for a 19-year-old, mentally retarded high school senior named David. David wanted to swim on the varsity team, but Connecticut Inter-Scholastic Association Conference ruled him ineligible because he was 19. Athletic directors and principals across the state joined hands to fight the Trumbull position, arguing that it would not be wise to let David swim.

David's articulate, dedicated parents were prepared to fight the school district and the state all by themselves. But, sensing the district's compassion, they persuaded the district to battle the state's athletic bureaucracy. The Trumbull lawyer and his supportive law firm took the case on pro bono, and Trumbull won in the local court and on appeal in the United States circuit court. The district was prepared to proceed all the way to the U.S. Supreme Court when the state athletic association realized it was backing a loosing cause and withdrew. Press coverage of the case cast a favorable light on the Trumbull School District and strengthened the administration's hand in dealing with other special education matters.

In general, parents of special-needs students are well aware that school districts have limited funding. They just want to be assured that districts are doing as much as they can to support their children. With patience and knowledge, a middle ground can usually be reached. Administrators who are prepared to suggest a range of alternatives and are willing to negotiate—and who are aided by an expert, capable lawyer—will be the most successful at controlling costs while satisfying concerned parents.

In this climate, where demands on school facilities constantly change and inexorably increase, it is incumbent on architects to become as knowledgeable as possible about all the issues affecting school design, to stay abreast of regulatory changes, and to keep school officials informed regarding how state and local mandates and case-law decisions will impact design, construction, and associated costs. Most of all, though, architects must counsel patience—and must do their part to help administrators prepare for the long, and occasionally difficult, road ahead, as our society strives to meet its obligations to special-needs students.

Chapter 18

Harmony in Value Engineering
by Marcia T. Palluzzi, LA

At the onset of any building project, all parties seek to create an environment that inspires. Often the process is tempered by practical, fiscal, and/or political challenges. It is during such controversies that value is established and inspiration becomes visible. Value engineering is the manifestation of the balance between priority and constructability.

Value engineering is most successful when it is fully integrated into the design process. It involves more than just changing or removing building materials or program functions. In fact, it involves seeing the path to the finished project in new ways. It is the component that makes the intangible tangible, often by creating a compromise between an idea and an affordable solution. Our beliefs about money and our understanding of the construction process work hand in hand in the value engineering process.

Our beliefs about money, and especially the voter's beliefs as revealed by the referendum process, can dramatically impact the course of the design process. Perceived need and actual need can be two very different things. It is essential that the building committee and board of education, working in conjunction with the architect, craft a financial strategy plan while the schematic building design is under development. Such a plan should include a communications strategy for gaining voter understanding, acceptance, and support of the project. (See Chapter 19, "Passing Your School Referendum," in this book.) It should also include an analysis of state reimbursement potential, a compilation of possible rebates for energy-efficient systems, and an assessment of the current labor market, availability of building materials, and the timing of similar projects in the region.

Oftentimes, value engineering decisions are made early on, during conception of the project. Expenditures on administrative office space, extensive parking areas, and large athletic complexes are frequently eliminated at the start before other cost options are investigated.

The conception period of a project is, in fact, a critical time in the value engineering process. Feasibility studies, often part of the conception process, provide a valuable analysis of potential paths that a project can take. The decisions to rehabilitate, build additions, or construct a completely new facility all have different cost implications. Consideration of facility needs, enrollment projections, state reimbursement, and energy rebates are some specific factors affecting the design.

Judgments related to initial cost versus long-term durability must be determined in the value engineering process. Balancing these two factors and making related decisions requires clear communication about the cost of materials, maintenance, and life-cycle of the products. For example, it is common to use dry wall instead of masonry on interior walls although the use of masonry is probably more cost-effective over the long run. Floor finishes, particularly in the cafeteria and hallways, will stand up longer and be easier to maintain if they are of high quality. The dollars spent to strip and wax low-grade finishes would in many cases probably more than pay for an upgrade.

Such decisions can also significantly impact the health and welfare of the individuals who will occupy the building. Lighting and acoustical treatments significantly impact vision and hearing. Improperly diffused ceiling lights can obscure lighting on computer screens, causing eyestrain or headaches. Improper computer furniture will affect posture, causing neck aches or backaches or even serious repetitive strain injuries. Acoustical treatments in a band room are critical to preventing damage to musicians' eardrums.

Another approach to reducing costs involves the re-evaluation of needs. Prioritizing the inclusion of certain spaces or reducing the sizes of critical spaces will bring the costs down. Compromising on the spaces or storage areas within the school can, however, have a large impact on the functioning and management of the facility. Cutting back on space is often the first strategy pursued because it is difficult to quantify the value of additional space. At this point in the space-adjustment process it is extremely important to obtain input from the Board of Education and knowledgeable educators to understand any related impact on student learning potential.

Lastly, the building systems should come under scrutiny. Heating and ventilation systems improperly distributed, balanced, and filtered will produce an unhealthy building with dirty ducts and/or hot-cold spots. Leaving air conditioning out of portions of a building will affect year-round building usage. But large, expensive facilities should be able to be used throughout the year. Also relevant in a discussion of mechanical systems is the opportunity to save money on operating the building through energy-efficient equipment. Although such equipment is costly, rebates from utility companies are often available.

So when and where do we value engineer a project? Ideally, it begins to occur during the conception of the project and has continues from there. It is clearly a collaborative process, which must balance need, funding, and creativity into a harmonious whole. Conscious effort to be aware of the cost estimating and financial strategic plan for the building will forestall surprises during the bidding process. Rather then pulling easily calculated items out of the equation, value engineering must be based on sound planning and design considerations. Time spent to gather data, communicate findings, and discuss priorities will pay off in the long run. Educated, "quality" decisions—made in a collaborative fashion—have the best chance of being cost-effective and providing the best learning environment for the student of tomorrow.

Chapter 19

Passing Your School Referendum: Community Support Is Based on Credibility

By Patricia A. Myler, AIA

Gaining the support of the community to fund a school project is a challenging task, particularly in transitional economic times. A referendum campaign, much like a school building itself, has to be carefully designed, because success does not happen by accident. The time and energy invested in planning, organizing, and running a campaign will be rewarded with the support of the community and a positive referendum vote.

It has been our experience that a well-designed and implemented communications program and campaign plan goes a long way toward achieving that support. The following is an outline of the referendum campaign process as it should generally occur. This process has to be customized, however, to address the distinctive needs of a particular community.

Designing the Campaign

The Project Architect. The architect is a critically important member of the referendum campaign team. The school district needs the expertise and technical guidance of an architectural firm—one specializing in school design and construction—to prepare the necessary design and other documents for presentations and public forums. In addition, an experienced architecture firm can lead the whole team through the referendum process by sharing knowledge gained in similar referendums in other communities.

This guidance is extremely important. The questions raised by the project's opponents, by its supporters, and by those voters who remain undecided must be answered professionally and completely to build the credibility necessary for victory.

Designing the Message. The target audience—those voters who are pro-education—must be identified, understood, and their electoral strength assessed. Research must be done into past campaigns and town referendums to determine the number of votes needed to win. The campaign team should utilize public hearings, focus groups, and questionnaires to identify voter issues and concerns.

Strong, organized opposition is often the primary factor in defeating a referendum. It is therefore critical to identify who is against the project and to determine why they oppose it and what alternatives they might support. Proposals should be structured to neutralize the opposition's arguments and to minimize surprises by predicting their reaction.

The Communications Subcommittee should be designated. It has the difficult task of sorting through all the information gathered and selecting three or four key facts that address the voters' major questions and clearly differentiate the arguments in support of the proposal from those of the opposition. The message needs to be simple and consistently repeated for voters to absorb the information. The need for the project, the benefit it will bring to the community, alternative options offered for consideration, tax implications, and the problems raised by doing nothing—all these should be addressed as part of the message.

The members of the Communications Committee—rather than the architect, district officials, or building committee members, who may be perceived to have a bias—should be the key deliverers of the message. Frequent committee meetings will be required to coordinate the content of the message and ensure consistency in its delivery.

Timing. The campaign should be initiated at least two to three months before the scheduled referendum date. This period is needed to design the campaign, and disseminate the necessary information to the voters. When the referendum is scheduled is extremely important to its success. The referendum should not coincide with municipal votes, nor should it occur during the summer months. During the summer, families with school-age children go on vacation, and low voter turnout—especially among those with the greatest stake in the project's success—can lead to defeat. Also, part-time summer residents may be less likely to support educational bond issues.

Getting the Message Out. The campaign has to determine the best mix of tools for communicating its message. A variety of communication tools are available, including paid advertising (print and broadcast), free media, direct mail, telephone banks, literature drops, neighborhood "walk and talks," public speaking, and letters to the editor.

Available resources will vary, but they can include volunteers, private funding, and business donations of materials, phone banks, meeting space, and free advertising. The committee must evaluate the available resources and develop a strategy to maximize their utilization.

Campaigns utilizing private funding are likely to be subject to strict regulation, and the committee may even have to register as a Political Action Committee (PAC). In most states, a guide to campaign financing is available from the state elections enforcement commission. There are also limitations on the role of public officials and consultants hired with public funds (including the architect) in the referendum process, and these must be fully understood to avoid conflict with these regulations.

The architect should prepare visual materials including site and floor plans, elevations, renderings, models, and CAD-generated animations. These graphic materials can be used in conjunction with a message developed to "tell the story." Posters and flyers can be developed for posting, mailing, and handing out. Local cable TV stations will provide free airtime to present the plans and animations and to broadcast discussions about the project. The campaign should also make the best use of press releases to local media, organize writing campaigns of letters to the editor, and sponsor public presentations and person-to-person neighborhood "walk and talks."

The support of the local press is immensely valuable. Endorsements by local media gain votes.

Phone banks are another important communication tool. It is desirable to have a location with multiple phone lines. Here, volunteers can call voters who belong to the targeted segments and deliver a carefully scripted message. This tool can be utilized at the initiation of the campaign as an information-gathering exercise, and again later on to remind the pro-education voters to get out and vote.

Implementing the Campaign

Phase 1: Educating the Voter. The Education Phase of a Referendum Process is a necessary first step. This phase brings issues within the school district to the public's attention, thus establishing "the need."

Establishing the Need. It is essential that the needs are established and communicated in order to solicit community support for a potential solution. It is equally important for the school district to understand the perceptions of their "customers" (administrators, teachers, parents, students, community, and the taxpayers). There must be an up-front commitment to understand these customers' points of view before any attempt is made to engage their support.

Demographic Research. Questionable demographic research can lead to diminished support for public education. The shrinking number of school-age children in the late 1960s and early 1970s led to school closures in many communities. With schools either closed or outdated there is a shortage of classroom and learning space. The public's recollection of this history must be addressed when projects are put forth for renovations, additions, or new schools. The proper demographic research must be executed to establish a credible database for future planning.

Community Relations. The public schools' relationship with the public does not begin with the development of the referendum process. Schools must develop and implement a long-range approach to optimize the daily interactions with their customers, and to solidify a supportive and informed contingency. Perceptions of a school or an entire district cannot be reversed within a relatively short referendum campaign. These beliefs about a school system, whether or not accurate or deserved, can account for much of what happens inside the voter booth.

Phase 2: The Campaign—Get the Story Out! Getting the story out to voters begins with a Referendum Workshop, or Campaign Kickoff Meeting, in which the campaign process is defined and the design of the campaign plan is initiated.

During this initial meeting, the campaign leadership positions are identified and the associated responsibilities defined. Appointments are made to each of the following campaign leadership positions:

- Campaign Chairperson
- Volunteer Coordinators for Research, Neighborhood Distribution, Phone Banks, and Business Support
- Communications Coordinator

Subcommittees are established to work with each campaign leader, and volunteers sign up for subcommittees. Assignments are made to initiate the research tasks for each subcommittee. The schedule and tasks are reviewed for production of a detailed campaign plan.

Table 19.1. Campaign Leadership Positions

Title	Responsibilities
I. Campaign Chairperson	1. Serves as chief spokesperson for the campaign.
	2. Administers the agreed-upon campaign plan.
	3. Chairs the Campaign Leadership Committee.
II. Volunteer Coordinators	
Research Coordinator	1. Researches targeted pr-education groups, including parents', PTA, and community groups. Cross-references target groups against voter registration lists.
	2. Researches past referendum results.
Neighborhood Distribution Coordinator	1. Identifies most effective neighborhood drop locations.
	2. Identifies most effective public distribution areas.
	3. Organizes and coordinates volunteers for the activities above.
	4. Coordinates timing of activities with the campaign plan.
Phone Bank Coordinator	1. Arranges for phone bank location(s).
	2. Organizes and coordinates volunteers for phone bank(s). Coordinates volunteers with the Neighborhood Distribution subcommittee.
	3. Coordinates timing of activities with the campaign plan.
Business Support Coordinator	1. Solicits support of local business.
	2. Coordinates placement of posters and flyers with the campaign plan.
III. Communication Coordinators	
Community Presentations Coordinator	1. Coordinates community presentations with the campaign plan.
	2. Designs presentations to incorporate the campaign plan.
Message Development Coordinator	1. Works with subcommittee to develop and refine key messages to be incorporated into campaign plan.
	2. Plans and develops press releases, reflecting the key messages.
Letters to the Editor Coordinator	1. Develops letter drafts based on the key campaign messages.
	2. Organizes and coordinates volunteers for letter-writing.
	3. Coordinates timing of letter placement with campaign plan.

Table 19.2 shows how you might design a volunteer sign-up sheet for the various subcommittees.

Tables 19.2. Sample Subcommittee Sign-Up Sheet

Please check off the subcommittee you would be interested in working on.

			Research	Neighborhood Distribution	Phone Bank
Name	Telephone	Email	Chairperson: _____	Chairperson: _____	Chairperson: _____

Table 19.3 presents a sample schedule for a two-month (March/April) campaign for a referendum scheduled for early May.

Table 19.3. Campaign Schedule

Task	3/3	3/10	3/17	3/24	3/31	4/07	4/14	4/21	4/28	5/5
Community Presentations										
Develop list										
Neighborhood Drops										
Message 1										
Message 2										
Message 3										
Message 4										
Message 5										
Public Distribution										
Letters to the Editor										
Draft letters										
Message 1										
Message 2										
Message 3										
Message 4										
Message 5										
Press Releases										
School Tour										
Cable TV Show										
Phone Bank										
Call pro-ed voters										
Research										
Identify pro-ed target										
Compare voter list										
ID opposition message										
Develop Campaign Message										
Flyers										
Posters										
Other Campaign Materials*										

* Other campaign materials might include poster boards for presentations (including floor plans, elevations), models, PowerPoint presentations, computer-generated video fly-through,
and so on.

Once the campaign plan has been developed, volunteers have signed up, and the schedule has been set, it's time to begin implementing the campaign. Here are some of the steps you'll need to follow:

Step 1: Identify the Target Groups and Assess Their Electoral Strength

- Research past campaigns and town referendums. Based on past referendum history, establish the number of votes needed to win (50 percent of the number likely to vote plus 1).
- Identify the target groups or voter segments most likely to support the referendum.
- Identify undecided and opponent voters.
- To determine the electoral strength of the target group, transfer lists of voters likely to support the referendum to the voting lists. This crossed-referenced list will serve as the basis for designing the communications program.
- Call identified "yes" voters.
- Maintain up-to-date voting records.

Step 2: Design an Effective Campaign Message

- Find out what the voters think and what they want to know. Based on feedback from public forums, newspaper articles and editorials, surveys, and general discussions, develop a list of the most important questions, issues, and concerns.
- Differentiate the arguments of the opposition. Determine who opposes the project and why they oppose it and what they might support as an alternative. Structure the proposal to neutralize the opponent's arguments and to minimize surprises by predicting the opponents' reactions.
- Keep the message simple and concise. Select three or four key facts that address the voters' major questions. The simple, concise message needs to be repeated consistently in order for voters to absorb the information.

Step 3: Determine the Mix of Tools to Communicate the Campaign Message

- Select communications tools based on the number of votes needed to win and their location, the message being communicated, and the availability of resources, (final and human).
- You may want to use any or all of the following communications tools:

  - Paid advertising—print and broadcast
  - Paid advertising—outdoor media
  - Free media
  - Direct mail
  - Phone banks
  - Mailers
  - Flyers
  - Newsletters
  - Press releases
  - Press interviews
  - Press conferences with TV, radio, newspapers

- Student participation
- Tours through existing, inadequate facilities
- Literature drops
- Neighborhood "walks and talks"
- Letters to the editor
- Public presentations to different groups (including the Board of Education, PTA/PTO, general public, students, media, town council)
- Email bursts
- A referendum website

Conclusion:

Looking Ahead

About the future one can never say the final word. And so this conclusion isn't a "conclusion" (in the sense of something final) at all. The only sensible way to "conclude" a book about the future is to look ahead, with openness, to the changes the future will bring.

In the years ahead, Americans will continue to focus on the nature and quality of our public education system, debating and experimenting with ways of strengthening the educational experience we give our children and improving the preparation they receive for entering the worlds of college, work, adult relationships, parenting, and citizenship. To accommodate new educational technologies and new approaches to schooling (undoubtedly including some that we cannot now predict), we must design schools to be as flexible as possible. But it's equally clear that our own thinking about what flexibility *is* and how it can best be achieved must also continue to evolve.

To respond effectively to the changes the future may bring, we must ourselves be willing to change our thinking, our strategies, and our priorities. This is a potentially endless task, and one that we—as designers, educators, parents, and citizens—should welcome. In concluding this book, we look forward to publishing further editions, in which the thinking we express here is refined, corrected, augmented, expanded—*changed* in ways that address the ongoing changes in American education, society, and culture.

We believe that our long experience in designing the full range of public education facilities provides us with insights that may be of value to middle school, high school, specialized school, and community college educators and administrators, as well. The other books in the Schools of the Future series are intended to serve these audiences: *The Middle School of the Future* and *The High School of the Future* are being published simultaneously with this volume; *Magnet and Charter Schools of the Future* and *Community Colleges of the Future* will appear in 2004 and 2005, respectively.

Finally, we mean what we say, throughout this book, when we speak of the value of collaboration and democratic process in school planning, design, and construction. It's our consistent experience as designers that thinking gets better and solutions become more effective as participation in the design process widens and grows. We therefore invite you, our readers, to participate in the making of future editions of this book. If there's anything you wish to respond to—anything we've missed, or overemphasized, or gotten wrong (or gotten right)—we'd very much like to hear from you. Contact us through our website, <www.fletcherthompson.com>.

Sources Cited

Barth, Roland S. 2001. *Learning by Heart.* Alexandria, Va.: Jossey-Bass.

Chicago Public Schools. 2000/2001. *Big Shoulders/Small Schools: The Chicago Public Schools Design Competition, 2000/2001 Competition Program.*

Connecticut Association of Public School Superintendents. 2002. "Technology Summit 2001: Visions and Beliefs." (White paper.) January.

Dillon, Sam. 2002. "Heft of Students' Backpacks Turns Into Textbook Battle." *New York Times.* December 24.

Franklin Hill & Associates. 1998. "The Metamorphosis of School Design." *The High School Magazine* (National Association of Secondary School Principals), May/June.

GAO (United States General Accounting Office). 1995. *School Facilities: Condition of America's Schools, February 1995.* GEO/HEHS-95-61. To access this and other GAO reports online, go to www.access.gpo.gov/su_docs/aces/aces160.shtml.

Gross, Jane. 2003. "What's Big, Yellow and Humiliating? Full Lot at Greenwich High Means New Reality: The Bus." *New York Times.* January 27.

Lewis, L., et al. 1999. "Condition of America's Public Schools." *Education Statistics Quarterly,* fall.

New York City Department of Health, Bureau of Environmental and Occupational Disease Epidemiology. "Guidelines on Assessment and Remediation of Fungi in Indoor Environments." 2000?. Published on the Web, at www.ci.nyc.ny.us/html/doh/html/epi/moldrpt1.html.

Pinker, Steven. 2003. "How to Get Inside a Student's Head." *New York Times.* January 31.

Seep, Benjamin, et al. 2000. *Classroom Acoustics: A Resource for Creating Learning Environments with Desirable Listening Conditions.* Melville, NY: Acoustical Society of America, Technical Committee on Architectural Acoustics.

Sterling, Bruce. 2002. *Tomorrow Now: Envisioning the Next Fifty Years.* New York: Random House.

Sustainable Buildings Industry Council. 2001. *High Performance School Buildings: Resourcer and Strategy Guide.* Washington, DC.

Winter, Greg. 2003. "Gates Foundation Providing $31 Million for Small Schools." *New York Times.* February 26.

Contributors

Edwin T. Merritt, Ed.D., is Director of Educational Planning & Research for Fletcher-Thompson, Inc. Over his 29-year career as a school superintendent (in three different districts), Ted Merritt was involved in more than 25 new construction, renovation, and major maintenance projects. A futurist and an expert on educational technology, he currently serves as a consultant on technology planning for the Connecticut State Department of Education. Mr. Merritt has received many awards, including the Connecticut State Superintendents' Golden Shield Award for Exemplary Service (1999), the General Connecticut Coast YMCA "Strong Kids Builder" Award (1999), the Bridgeport Regional Leader of the Year Award (1998), and the Rotary Club's Paul Harris Fellowship (1998), and he has been a National and State Parent/Teachers' Association Honoree (1993, 1999). He has written for *American School & University* and *School Business Affairs,* among other publications.

James A. Beaudin, AIA, is the Principal of Fletcher-Thompson, Inc.'s Educational Practice Group. Over his career, Mr. Beaudin has been involved in the design of almost 100 schools in 45 communities—for a total of more than 10 million square feet of public and private school construction. Since 1990, the firm, under his direction, has created more than 7.5 million square feet of educational space, with a combined construction value in excess of $500 million and comprising projects for every educational level, from pre-kindergarten through high school. Besides new construction, projects directed by Mr. Beaudin have included renovations, code-compliance improvements, system-wide studies, and educational programming and specification development. Under his leadership, Fletcher-Thompson's Educational Practice Group has received numerous awards and other recognition. Articles authored or co-authored by Mr. Beaudin have appeared in *American School & University, Facilities Design & Management, School Business Affairs,* and *School Planning & Management* magazines.

Jeffrey A. Sells, AIA, is the Design Leader of Fletcher-Thompson, Inc.'s Educational Practice Group, responsible for the design approach on all of the firm's educational projects. He has designed new elementary and high school buildings as well as additions and renovations of elementary, middle, high, and magnet schools in districts throughout Connecticut. He has also designed college and university facilities, including the Thomas Dodd Archives and Research Center at the University of Connecticut. His work has been featured in professional publications and has won numerous awards and special recognition. His written work has appeared in *Engineering News-Record, School Business Affairs, American School and University,* and *The CABE Journal,* and he has been a collaborator on, or primary contributor to, articles for *Contract* and *Building Design & Construction* magazines and the *Connecticut Post.*

Richard S. Oja, AIA, is a Senior Project Manager at Fletcher-Thompson, Inc. For more than 12 years, he has managed public school projects, from project inception through programming, design, bidding, construction, and post-occupancy evaluation. He has worked on a full range of educational facilities, from small elementary schools to major suburban and urban high schools. He has focused on schools' indoor environmental quality issues, giving presentations and publishing articles, including a recent piece in *Facilities Design & Management,* on the topic.

Karen Fairbanks, a Partner at Marble Fairbanks Architects, received her Master of Architecture degree at Columbia University, where she won the AIA Medal, the William Kinne Fellowship, and the Fred L. Liebman Book Award and was the representative for Columbia University in the SOM Traveling Scholarship Competition. She has taught at Columbia University since 1989 and is currently the Director of the Barnard and Columbia Colleges Architecture Program. She was a New York Foundation for the Arts Fellow in Architecture in 1988 and 1994.

Scott Marble, a Partner at Marble Fairbanks Architects, received his Master of Architecture degree from Columbia University, where he was awarded the AIA Award and the William Kinne Fellowship. Scott has taught at Columbia University Graduate School of Architecture, Planning, and Preservation since 1987, serving as the Coordinator of Graduate Studies from 1992 through 1994. Since 1995 he has served as the editor of *Abstract,* the catalog of the Graduate School of Architecture, Planning, and Preservation of Columbia University. In 1987 he co-edited the book *Architecture and Body*, published by Rizzoli. Scott was a New York Foundation for the Arts Fellow in Architecture in 1994. In 1992 he was a winner in the Young Architects Forum sponsored by the Architectural League of New York.

Marble Fairbanks Architects (MFA) is the New York City–based practice of Scott Marble and Karen Fairbanks. The two began collaborating in 1990 and have worked on a wide range of residential, commercial, and institutional projects. In January 2002 the firm received a P/A Award (Progressive Architecture Award) by *Architecture Magazine* for its project for the Chicago Public Schools. The Chicago Athenaeum selected three MFA projects to receive American Architecture Awards for 2001. A recent project, Open Loft, was published in the September 2000 issue of *Architectural Record* as one of the Record Interiors for the year 2000. In September 1999, MFA's design for ticket booths at the Museum of Modern Art was one of 21 schemes (out of more than 900 entries) to receive an award by *The Architectural Review* in an open international competition for architects under 45. Among other recent honors and awards, the Architectural League of New York selected Scott Marble and Karen Fairbanks as Emerging Voices in 1998. In 1996, Scott Marble and Karen Fairbanks were selected for "Forty Under Forty," an award recognizing the top 40 designers and architects under the age of 40. In 1994, 1996, 1997, 1999, and 2001, MFA won Design Awards from the New York Chapter of the American Institute of Architects. The Architectural League of New York selected MFA's work for exhibition at the Urban Center in New York City as part of the Young Architects Forum in 1992. In 1991, MFA was selected as one of five finalists (out of more than 600 offices worldwide) competing in the Nara [Japan] Convention Hall International Design Competition. This project has been exhibited throughout the world and was on view at the Museum of Modern Art in New York as part of its Preview Series in 1992–1993.

Barry M. Blades, ASLA, Principal of Blades & Goven, LLC, has over 20 years of experience in the fields of landscape architecture, site planning and environmental planning and analysis. He has served as designer, project manager, and/or principal-in-charge on numerous elementary, middle, and high school projects throughout Connecticut. He performed contract administration services for New Milford High School, which included the development of an extensive athletic field complex. He has also recently completed schematic design and regulatory approvals for additions and renovations to the Wilton High School campus. Along with his extensive experience in working with school building committees and town commissions, Mr. Blades has been responsible for the processing and acquisition of numerous environmental permits from regulatory agencies. He has also assisted educational clients with feasibility studies and site analyses/evaluations for potential school projects.

Blades & Goven, LLC, is a Shelton, Connecticut–based firm offering consulting landscape architectural, site planning, and related design services to clients in the public and private sectors. The firm was established in 1996 through the merger of the independent practices of the firm's two principals, Barry Blades and Earl Goven.

Joseph G. Costa, AIA, an Associate and Project Manager with Fletcher-Thompson, Inc., has more than 18 years of professional experience. His project management duties, on a diverse range of project types, have included full project responsibility from conceptualization to implementation, manpower allocation and budgeting, cost analyses, scheduling, contract negotiation, consultant administration and coordination, construction documentation, and construction administration.

Daniel Davis, AIA, a Senior Design Architect with Fletcher-Thompson, Inc., has more than 20 years of experience designing a broad range of project types, including educational, institutional, commercial, corporate and industrial facilities. He is a professor in the University of Hartford's Department of Architecture, where he teaches architectural history and design. His architectural writings have appeared in a variety of publications, ranging from local newspapers to national professional journals. His projects have been published in leading architectural magazines and have won prestigious design awards.

L. Gerald Dunn, R.A., a Senior Design Architect with Fletcher-Thompson, Inc., has extensive experience in designing performance centers, retail/entertainment facilities, schools, hotels, and mixed-use projects, as well as in master planning large-scale developments worldwide. He served as Director of Urban Design for the Disney Development Company in Paris and as Principal Concept Architect for Disney's Animal Kingdom in DisneyWorld, Florida. Mr. Dunn has also been the design architect for major commercial and cultural facilities in the United States and internationally.

John D. Jenney, Construction Support Administrator for Fletcher-Thompson, Inc., has for 19 years played an active role in the design and construction industry in positions ranging from lead carpenter to project manager. Mr. Jenney's responsibilities have included supervising and coordinating site work, developing project cost estimates and monitoring project costs, developing in-house designs for building modifications, establishing work schedules, and coordinating activities with customers, contractors, and company personnel.

Julie A. Kim, AIA, a Project Manager with Fletcher-Thompson, Inc., has extensive experience in commercial, institutional, and educational design. Recent work includes a new K–8 school in New Haven, Connecticut, and pre-referendum studies for school projects in the towns of Guilford, Connecticut, and Rye, New York.

Patricia A. Myler, AIA, is Director of Pre-K through Grade 12 Facilities and an Associate at Fletcher-Thompson, Inc. Since joining the firm in 1995, she has served as a studio leader and project manager and is currently Director of the firm's Hartford, Connecticut, office, focusing on educational projects that have ranged from feasibility studies for elementary, middle, high, and magnet schools; to additions and renovations; to new primary, magnet, middle, and high schools. She has also provided pre-referendum consulting services to several Connecticut school districts. She is the co-author of a recent *School Business Affairs* article, "Going Up?," on the feasibility of vertical expansions of existing school facilities.

JoAnne Nardone, Ed.D., is the Principal of Milton School in Rye, New York (a K-5 National School of Excellence). Formerly, she served as Assistant to the Superintendent of the Hendrick Hudson School District and, before that, as a Program Specialist in the office of the Chancellor of the New York City Public Schools and as District Director of Foreign Languages and English as a Second Language. She has taught Spanish and Italian to grades 7 through 12 and ESL and Bilingual Education to grades K through 6. She holds a doctorate in Educational Administration from Columbia University.

John C. Oliveto, P.E., Principal and Director of Construction Support Services at Fletcher Thompson, is responsible for administering the firm's construction administration assignments; he serves as project field representative on select projects. He is also responsible for a design phase reviews aimed at improving the quality and efficiency of construction documents. He has performed construction support services for a number of Connecticut educational projects, including additions and renovations to the Eleanor B. Kennelly School in Hartford and renovations to the Six to Six Early Childhood Magnet School in Bridgeport.

Marcia T. Palluzzi, LA, is registered landscape architect. While she was at Fletcher-Thompson, Inc., her work focused on the pre-planning process, programming, land-use studies, and regulatory approvals for educational and other projects.

Robert J. Poletto, P.E., served as Fletcher Thompson's Chief Mechanical Engineer.

Edward Weber, P.E., an Associate in Fletcher Thompson's Construction Support Services department, has over 16 years of experience in the construction field. As a field representative, his responsibilities include interpretation and enforcement of contract documents, establishing standards of acceptability, judging contractor performance, issuing certified authorization of payments to the contractor, making special inspections to determine the date of completion, and informing the owner of the status of the work. He also monitors construction loans and/or joint ventures between lending institutions and contractors/developers through detailed review of drawings and specifications, review of contractors' budgets and project schedules, and job site inspections.

Photo Credits

Introduction, page xxv: Robert Benson Photography

Chapter 1, page 3: Lampel Photography

Chapter 2, page 9: Fletcher-Thompson, Inc.

Chapter 3, page 21: (clockwise) Robert Benson Photography; Marble
Fairbanks rendering; Fletcher Thompson rendering; Woodruff/
Brown Photography
page 22: David Sundberg/Esto (top); Robert Benson Photography (bottom)
page 23: David Sundberg/Esto (top & middle); Robert Benson Photography (bottom)
page 28: Andrew Krochko (top); Woodruff Brown Photography (bottom)

Chapter 4, page 31: Woodruff/Brown Photography

Chapter 5, page 41: Woodruff/Brown Photography

Chapter 6, page 49: Lampel Photography

Chapter 7, page 55: Woodruff/Brown Photography

Chapter 8, page 67: David Sundberg/Esto

Chapter 9, page 71: Woodruff/Brown Photography

Chapter 12, page 97: James D'Addio Photographer

Chapter 13, page 109: Lampel Photography

Chapter 14, page 113: Lampel Photography

Chapter 15, page 119: Woodruff/Brown Photography

Chapter 16, page 125: David Sundberg/Esto

Chapter 18, page 141: Lampel Photography

Chapter 19, page 143: Woodruff/Brown Photography